RUHLMANN
Master of Art Deco

RUHLMANN
Master of Art Deco

Florence Camard

with 487 illustrations, 67 in colour

Thames and Hudson

Translated from the French by David Macey

First published in Great Britain in 1984 by
Thames and Hudson Ltd, London

Reprinted 1993

Printed and bound in Italy

Contents

To Jules Deroubaix
cabinet-maker and faithful co-worker of
Jacques-Emile Ruhlmann; his testimony
and his archives, bequeathed to him by
Madame Ruhlmann, have made this
book possible

Ruhlmann in about 1928; 'A little man with bright eyes peering
out from behind thick tortoiseshell-rimmed spectacles.'
Photograph: Laure Albin-Guillot.

Ruhlmann fishing for trout in about 1930. Jules Deroubaix made the fly box designed by Ruhlmann himself in macassar ebony.

Fisherman on the Adour, sketches by Ruhlmann.

s. l'Adour

Modernity and the cult of the past. Attempts to explain the eclipse of Art Nouveau in terms of its naturalistic and curvilinear excesses tend to obscure the fact that French society was stagnant and had become trapped in a cult of the past.

In the transitional years leading up to 1914, only the couturiers Paul Poiret and Jacques Doucet showed any daring. In 1912, the latter auctioned his collection of eighteenth-century furniture, paintings and objets d'art in order to encourage young artists, but that was a very exceptional gesture.

The difficulties encountered by the Société des Artistes Décorateurs (founded in 1901) show the extent to which French aesthetic conservatism was an obstacle to artistic production. The SAD came up against a coalition of interests which compromised all its efforts. The turn-of-the-century enthusiasm for new lines had given way to a concern with profitability. Manufacturers exploited tried and tested forms. No longer able to create, architects preached prudence. Antiques dominated the market in a conformist society which had lost its sense of identity.

At the time when Jacques-Emile Ruhlmann made his debut in 1913, the situation was even more disturbing in that the artists and manufacturers of the Deutsche Werkbund were achieving spectacular results with a resolutely modern programme: 'German industrial artists understand that it is not simply a question of aesthetics, but a question of life and death. . . We have to create an art industry that is capable of becoming a world-wide industry.' Karl Scheffer made no secret of the fact that Germany's main ambition was to capture the traditional clientele of the furniture-makers of the Faubourg Saint-Antoine. The Werkbund's offensive provoked a healthy reaction on the part of the French authorities.[1]

Official catalogue for the German section in the Exposition Internationale, Brussels, 1910.

In 1912, the Chamber of Deputies voted to hold a major international exhibition designed to re-establish the threatened prestige of the French decorative arts. Only modern works were to be exhibited; no reproductions could be shown. Originally planned for 1915, the exhibition was postponed several times because of the war, and finally took place in 1925, as the Exposition Internationale des Arts Décoratifs et Industriels which gave its name to 'Art Déco'. It fulfilled all the organizers' expectations: attitudes had changed sufficiently for a new style to be fully accepted.

---

1 As of 1920, all the credits allotted to the Mobilier National were used to purchase contemporary works 'in order to combat the German and Austrian artisans who, even before the war, had captured the world market'. The Mobilier National collection of Ruhlmann includes two major pieces acquired in 1926: the macassar ebony corner cupboard and a sideboard in bur amboina-wood and ivory with *caillouté* veneering.

L'Illustration, 30 June 1928.

As Henri Clouzot recalled in 1928, 'Modern furniture was created by the artists themselves. They had to fly in the face of prevailing tastes, and it has taken them twenty years to gain public recognition. It might still be a matter of private patronage, were it not for the powerful intervention of the big department stores, which used the power of advertising to overcome public prejudices.'

A rational elitism. The First World War led to a rapid change in public attitudes. Norms and conventions were swept aside; technological change transformed everyday life; a modern decorative art was finally able to develop. A new bourgeoisie had emerged. It was open to artistic innovation and wanted to see the development of a new, contemporary art of living.

Report on the Tunis International Exhibition, 1911.

Furniture designers still recalled the failure of the previous generation, that of the 'Art for All' movement, which had tried to give the public furniture adapted to its needs. The critic Raymond Koechlin drew the following conclusions from its failure: 'The masses will always follow fashion. . . and the novelties they adopt will never be anything more than cheap imitations of models created by artists for the élite which sets the fashion.'

Art et Décoration, May 1921.

Jacques-Emile Ruhlmann has often been criticized for designing furniture solely for a wealthy clientele. But did he in fact have any alternative? In 1921, Maurice Dufrêne, who was responsible for organizing the Galeries Lafayette's 'Maîtrise' department, summed up the difficulties involved in vulgarization: 'Decorators do not work for the ''rich'' because they want to, or because they have no sense of social duty. They do so because they have no choice. In so far as he is an artist, the decorator can do what he likes. In so far as he is a businessman, he unfortunately has to do what he can. He creates for the people who ask him to do so.'

Ruhlmann was forced to adopt the same strategy.[2] The production of a piece of furniture accounted for almost half its cost price. The cost of producing designs, preparing for prestige exhibitions and paying his highly qualified staff left him with virtually no profit margins. His rehabilitation of the notion of luxury and his promotion of quality furniture were simply strategies to persuade the public to accept modern furniture rather than period pieces or reproductions.[3]

2 'New creations have never been made for the middle classes. They have always been made at the request of an élite which unsparingly gives artists the time and money needed for laborious research and perfect execution.' Cited, *L'Illustration*, 30 June 1930.
3 The *artistes décorateurs* were accused of indulging in experimentation for the sake of it, but found an eloquent defender in Jules Leleu: 'A writer's experiments cost only a little paper and ink. Those of Ruhlmann and his colleagues cost astronomical sums of money, but not at the customer's expense.'

From fashion to style. Throughout his career, Ruhlmann stressed the affinities and similarities between the art of the decorator and that of the couturier. If the decorators of the interwar period were to create, they, like the couturiers, had to have the backing of those who 'set the fashions'.

With its uniformity of taste and behaviour, modern consumer society gives the impression that fashion is no longer the distinctive mark of an 'élite', and the rhetoric of advertising helps to convey that impression. Sociologists, however, have discovered that the very institution which claims to abolish cultural inequality in fact does most to preserve it. 'Ideologically, the cult of the ephemeral connotes the privileges of the avant-garde. Up-to-date models are the preserve of the privileged classes.' By creating the illusion of a social mobility which does not in fact exist, fashion 'effects a compromise between the need for innovation and the need to preserve the underlying order unchanged'.

J. Baudrillard, *Traverse*, No. 2, 'Le Design'.

The empirical observations made by Ruhlmann himself immediately after the First World War anticipate the theories of modern sociology: 'The rationale for fashion is a desire for change and a desire to establish a hierarchy of wealth. A closed aristocracy of expensive objects is therefore made for the exclusive use of an élite. So far, the only pieces of furniture judged worthy of belonging to that aristocracy are antiques whose pedigree can be traced through auction catalogues – the ''stud books'' of the objet d'art.'

When he states that 'Like it or not, style is fashion. And the lower classes never set fashions!', he is not being paradoxical. Nor is he confusing the notions of fashion and style: fashion is often a necessary precondition for style, but it is never a sufficient precondition. Not all fashions give birth to a style, but an emergent style always begins by recycling taste and by making conventional 'good taste' look outdated.

Art et décoration, January 1920.

The couturier Paul Poiret shattered the sullen conformism of his contemporaries at just the right moment and therefore acted as a stimulus to the new artistic movement that developed after 1910. Ruhlmann himself followed the 'Boudoir or Studio' style established by Poiret for a while, but he wanted to do more than follow a never-ending sequence of fads and yearly changes of fashion. Paul Poiret had placed his inventiveness at the service of fashion, but Ruhlmann had higher and more far-reaching ambitions. His work belongs to the historical period in which what we now call 'style' was distilled and crystallized.

As for those who adopt a fashion, it cannot be denied that they are in part motivated by a desire to stand out from the crowd, as well as by a desire to support the artists they believe in. Others may have waited for the movement to gain official recognition (in the shape of the 1925

Exposition Internationale), but their support was also vital to the existence of the Art Déco style.

The twenties are the only period in which both buyers at auctions and dealers' customers turned away from antiques. Contemporary pieces made higher prices than earlier styles. Many different groups contributed to making this temporary but exceptionally widespread shift in taste possible: the great designers, the department stores, critics, the government, the initial admirers of the new style and, finally, those who rallied to it only when the battle had already been won.

Unique pieces and mass-produced furniture. The production of unique and personalized pieces of furniture can be seen as a practical corollary of Ruhlmann's strategy. When Guillaume Janneau asked him about the possibility of producing an edition of his models, he admitted: 'You've caught me off my guard. So far, I have never even thought of mass-producing my furniture. My own view is that we first have to win an élite which is still the arbiter of taste over to the new spirit, which is not to say that we should be thinking only of the élite.'

Formes nouvelles, programme nouveau, 1925.

By 1920, he was giving a clearer definition of the role of the creator and of the process of popularization. 'Just as a thoroughbred that is selected at great cost for pointless races ultimately helps to improve the working breed. . . the luxury object is a stallion which helps to improve the standard of mass-produced objects.' The big stores, all of which had set up dynamic modern art departments, played an important part, as they could adapt the innovations of the great decorators without distorting them. Many artists went through an apprenticeship in teamwork in them before setting up on their own. Ruhlmann himself was under no illusion about the furniture manufacturers of the Faubourg Saint-Antoine. That irreducible bastion 'will go on turning out imitations so long as influential people go on buying reproduction furniture. But once the new style conquers the élite, the Faubourg will immediately burn its old idols and flood the market with modern art *ad usum populi.*'

Art et décoration, January 1920.

Art et décoration, January 1920.

The rules for the 1925 exhibition confirmed his predictions: after a long polemic between decorators and manufacturers, all reproduction furniture was excluded. The period between 1925 and 1930 saw a spectacular, if not total, change in the attitudes of furniture manufacturers. And inevitably, a price had to be paid when the new fashion was no longer restricted to a small circle of initiates: plagiarism.[4]

4 In order to protect themselves against plagiarism, the *artistes décorateurs* set up a *chambre syndicale* in 1922. Its president, Charles Plumet, was instructed to draw up a protocol on artistic property and on the obligations incumbent upon manufacturers who wanted to produce editions of original models.

Ruhlmann could produce cheap and simple furniture and still remain true to himself (and did so for the Cité Universitaire), but the 'poor man's Ruhlmann' pieces turned out by some Paris workshops were simply forgeries. These pretentious and shoddily-made imitations debased the spirit of the originals by caricaturing them.

Did the success of the great decorators lead to a new conformism of taste? Unlike the avant-garde, they administered modernity in homeopathic doses and tamed the public without rushing matters. They expressed respect and admiration for their illustrious forerunners, but made no secret of their desire to oust them. As Jules Leleu once ironically remarked to admirers of antique furniture, 'It's a great asset to be no more; and when the dead compete with the living they don't play fair.'

Ruhlmann and Le Corbusier. It may seem paradoxical to compare two such different personalities. But in so far as we do have the analytical tools to compare the most famous decorator of the interwar period and one of the fathers of contemporary design, the parallel has both an historical and a premonitory value. Ruhlmann and Le Corbusier were champions of two different systems of ethics, of two different ideologies, and their polemic was not an individual matter. It was part of a wider polemic which is still relevant.

When he published *L'Art décoratif d'aujourd'hui* in 1924, the thirty-seven-year-old Le Corbusier was still an 'armchair architect'. He was also one of the few modernists in France to have any personal experience of the Munich Werkbund or any informed knowledge of the Weimar Bauhaus experiment. At a time when disputes between France and Germany were compromising the desire for a political rapprochement, these were both dubious recommendations.

Although he had had little opportunity to put his ideas into practice, Le Corbusier had to a large extent outlined his theoretical work in the journal *Esprit nouveau*, erecting functionalism into a system which turned the house into a 'machine for living' and furniture into 'equipment'.

Le Corbusier seemed to be an eccentric rather than a prophet. His predictions seemed too far removed from contemporary reality for them to come true in the foreseeable future, and his verbal excesses irritated or scandalized people rather than convincing them. Many people regarded even the possibility of his participation in the 1925 Exposition Internationale as undesirable, and, even though he did take part, thanks

Unfortunately, the charter proved impractical and did not prevent copies from being made. Pastiche antiques were replaced by pastiche Art Déco. In a sense, this meant that the style had finally been accepted, but for its creators it was a hollow victory.

to subsidies from an industrialist in Bordeaux, he was not fully accepted. Relegated to a marginal site and cut off behind fences, the Pavillon de l'Esprit Nouveau looked like an interloper. It was merely a *cellule d'habitation* and, not being integrated into any large unit like the 'Cité radieuse', simply looked like a futurist villa, a foil to the Hôtel du Collectionneur. It is easy to mock the obscurantism of earlier generations, but it is not in fact surprising that the public preferred Ruhlmann's style and luxury to Le Corbusier's rejection of decoration and his integration of metallic furniture into the architecture.

In many ways, Le Corbusier was the complete antithesis of Ruhlmann, not because he included him in his sarcastic comments about the 'buffoons who believe in decorative art', but because he regarded Ruhlmann as a perfect example of 'the mainstream of high-minded decorators who satisfy a cultivated clientele's taste for luxury', an obstacle to the architect's dream of replacing the proprieties with the law of enamel paint. Neither the pretensions to style, the excellence of the cabinet-making – a technique belonging to a different age – nor the 'devotion to fine materials which leads to hair-splitting' found any favour in his eyes. The impertinent and double-edged comment that 'I find the rare veneers as astonishing as humming-birds' appears to apply to a reproduction of a particularly precious table by Ruhlmann.

The polemic over the content of decorative art is in fact symptomatic of an ideological debate. Like the Bauhaus, Le Corbusier wanted everyone to have equal access to furniture. He wanted to find a functional solution to objective needs – seating, storage – by using standardized equipment reduced to the efficiency of 'a good servant who stands aside and leaves his master free'.

Whereas Ruhlmann exhibited sixty chairs and ninety armchairs, Le Corbusier showed three tubular prototypes. 'To tell the truth,' he stated, 'decorative art means equipment, beautiful equipment. We are not dealing with individual, arbitrary or eccentric cases; we are dealing with norms and creating model objects.'

Even before Le Corbusier invented his 'standards' in association with Charlotte Perriand and Jeanneret, other modernists such as Francis Jourdain, Eileen Gray and Pierre Chareau were putting a similar programme into effect and were furnishing interiors by stripping them. Their common aim was to disown the repertoire they had inherited from the past and which merely cluttered up apartments without resolving the problem of storage. The poetic terminology of the past itself suggested furniture with no specific function: *bonheur-du-jour, chiffonnier, vide-poche. . .*

Le Corbusier wanted to replace all these with metallic boxes inspired by the medieval coffer. Eileen Gray invented an ingenious system of drawers mounted on a vertical axis which opened up to form a 'staircase'. Pierre Chareau adapted the cabin trunk by adding a wrought-iron hinge.

It is often forgotten that Ruhlmann made his own contribution to the avant-garde as well as producing prestige furniture. In the 1929 Salon des Artistes Décorateurs, he exhibited a bookcase designed for a 'Viceroy of India' (a transparent disguise for the young Maharajah of Indore) consisting of standardized macassar ebony modules. These could be assembled at will and either stacked vertically or juxtaposed horizontally. They could be used to make a filing cabinet, a display case, a sideboard or a room-divider, depending upon whether the drop-leaf front was in glass or wood.

Standard and sign. The dogma of primary needs which is so dear to functionalism is a response to Le Corbusier's formula of 'standard needs, standard functions, standard objects, standard furniture', an empirical postulate which stresses only the use-value of the object.

Modern sociology demolishes this over-simplistic interpretation by showing that such utilitarian claims mask a coded differential relation: the 'sign-value' that underlies our behaviour. A true theory of objects and of consumption, we are told, cannot be based upon a theory of needs and of the satisfaction of needs. It must be based upon a theory of social performance and its meaning. Even though there is a physiological need for seating, there were never sufficient chairs for all the courtiers at Versailles simply because a chair functioned as a sign which embodied the subtle hierarchy of differences imposed by the king. Only Louis XIV and the princes of the blood royal had the right to sit down in public, and we know from Saint-Simon that obtaining even a stool represented an enviable distinction. In the eighteenth century, when ambitious people no longer had to appear at court, etiquette lost its magical power of constraint. The demand for comfort and intimacy, changes in women's dress and the hold of fashion in high society gave rise to an extraordinary variety of chairs for different settings and different circumstances. As a result, a logic of differences, and even minor differences, that had little to do with practical considerations developed. Ruhlmann's 150 models, all with minor variations between them, derive from a similar codified practice of extravagance, especially as each chair was named after its first purchaser.

'There is more to an object than its purpose, and it is that excess presence that gives it its prestige significance.' This comment is particularly applicable to pieces of furniture which ostentatiously display the social status of their owner. Thus, a silver-cabinet is used to display precious objects, even though it is less secure than a strong-box; bookcases replace shelves and become cabinets to display their owner's literary knowledge; bars and television sets are concealed behind rows of dummy books to give at least an appearance of culture. Similarly, the dressing-table is a complaisant aid to coquetry and presupposes the existence of a lady of leisure whose one desire is to please.

Being a rationalist, Ruhlmann believed that an elegant model was one which 'fulfilled needs as naturally and simply as possible'. But he also wanted his pieces to be accepted as aesthetic objects with an indexed social significance. They had that significance from the outset and still have it.

It seems unlikely that standard furniture ever succeeded in escaping the traps of fashion and human vanity. The functionalist utopia never became a reality. The daring housing policy needed for it to be realized simply did not exist in France in the thirties. It remained restricted to an élite who were close to the modernists. Standards designed for mass production were made on the basis of occasional commissions from sympathizers or patrons. No edition of Le Corbusier's famous chaise-longue was produced until twenty years after Thonet's prototypes had been shown. The audience of the Union des Artistes Modernes was too restricted for it to have any mass following, and it now looks like a caste phenomenon based upon culture if not wealth. Fashion popularized debased versions of Art Déco on a wide scale, but not the technological innovations which defied prevailing tastes, even though the influence of functionalism was apparent throughout the thirties, particularly in hybrid pieces using both wood and metal.

Ruhlmann's élitist strategy thus succeeded, whereas Le Corbusier's ambitious project of abolishing art as an aristocratic form of creation met with failure. Fifty years after the death of Ruhlmann, we are faced with the paradoxical situation in which functionalism has become commonplace, in which 'equipment' contributes to the depersonalization of our social and working environment, and in which contemporary designers are again working for a new aristocracy which enjoys the privileges of both money and culture. Thanks to Art Déco furniture and design, both Ruhlmann and Le Corbusier have been rehabilitated by the cyclical logic of fashion, 'the dominant system, the only system which has become truly universal and which governs the production and circulation of signs'.

J. Baudrillard, *Traverse*, No.2, 'Le Design'.

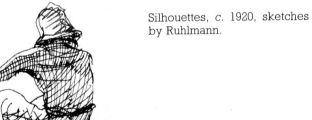

Silhouettes, *c.* 1920, sketches by Ruhlmann.

Sketch, 1910. Art Nouveau bed
and decorative motifs.

Studies for the Tibattant secretaire. Sketchbook 11, 1915.

RUHLMANN AS FURNITURE DESIGNER

Sketches. Sketching was a constant part of Ruhlmann's creative activity. His earliest sketches date from 1897, at which time he had just left school and cannot have known that he was to be an artist.

Until 1903, furniture studies are rare, and are mostly inspired by Art Nouveau. In contrast, there are a lot of sketches of everyday life: caricatures, portraits, genre scenes and landscapes. We know that, both before and after his military service, Ruhlmann frequented the workshops of Gevens, Stauffacher and Laberthe and we can assume that his masters encouraged his taste for drawing. Major changes came about after his marriage in 1907, and especially in 1913 when he decided to open a decorating and furnishing agency in addition to his painting and mirror-making business. Although most documents relating to the period 1907–1913 have been lost, many witnesses state that Ruhlmann always carried a sketchbook in which he would rapidly draw plans for furniture, motifs for carpets and assembly methods.

Some fifty of these documents survive.[1] For unexplained reasons, the sequence of sketchbooks breaks off in 1925, but it is unlikely that Ruhlmann ever gave up sketching. The loss of later notebooks is unfortunate in that it leaves us with an imperfect knowledge of the last eight years of Ruhlmann's life and of the process that led him to combine wood and non-conventional materials.

Most of the sketches date from between 1913 and 1919. He produced relatively few pieces of furniture during the war, but conceptually this was a very fertile period, the results of which would be seen in the twenties.

The artistic and documentary value of Ruhlmann's sketches did not escape contemporary critics. A selection of sketches was published with

Croquis de Ruhlmann. Collection documentaire d'art moderne, Paris, Albert Lévy, 1924.

a preface by Léon Moussinac, who stresses the fascination of 'discovering the origins and the development of such a personality, of studying different phases in his research and of going back to what one might call the original idea'. The fifty-two plates reproduce several hundred drawings, but it is to be regretted that they are not presented with more scientific rigour: the sketches are classified by genre, with no indication of their date or of whether or not they were ever executed.

1 Twenty-six of his sketchbooks were left to the Musée des Arts Décoratifs when Madame Ruhlmann died in 1959. Of the twenty-two left to Monsieur Deroubaix, eleven were presented to the Bibliothèque Nationale in 1973. Most are numbered, but it is not possible to establish any definite chronology, as the numbering was not introduced until about 1918 and does not cover the first part of the century.

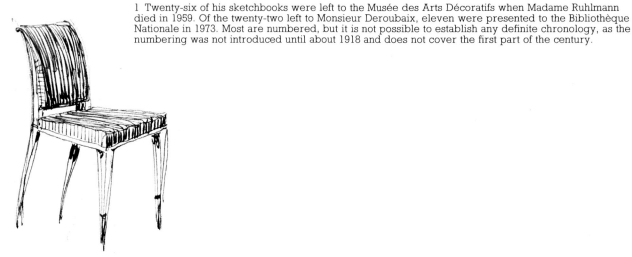

Sketch dated 1919. Sketchbook 28.

Studies for the Manqbéton chair with single back leg.

Fuseau dressing-table for the Hôtel du Collectionneur. Drawing by Ruhlmann, signed, annotated and dated.

A comparison between the finished pieces and the sketches does, however, show that the creative process always followed the same basic lines: the time gap between the initial idea for a piece of furniture and its execution can be as long as six to eight years; a variety of approaches are used to harmonize the various elements (structure, facing, support). As Moussinac remarks, 'The major interest of the sketches is that we find in them traces of the artist's hesitations, calculations and doubts. We can take part in the creative process.'

Thus, the three studies for Ruhlmann's Elysée sideboard show that his main concern was to balance the volume and the *caillouté* marquetry. The redundant and unusual shapes which appear in the sketches were eliminated. The somewhat baroque designs for a sideboard with multiple lobes were abandoned, only a few half-moon shapes being spared. The process of selection represents a movement towards increasing rigour and simplicity.

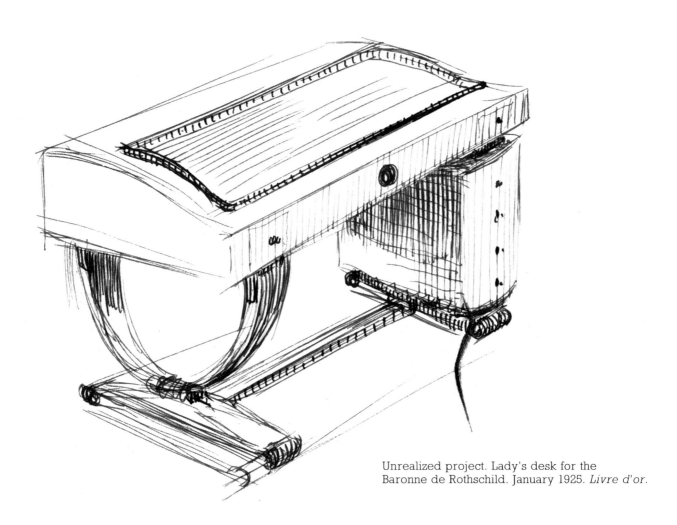

Unrealized project. Lady's desk for the
Baronne de Rothschild. January 1925. *Livre d'or*.

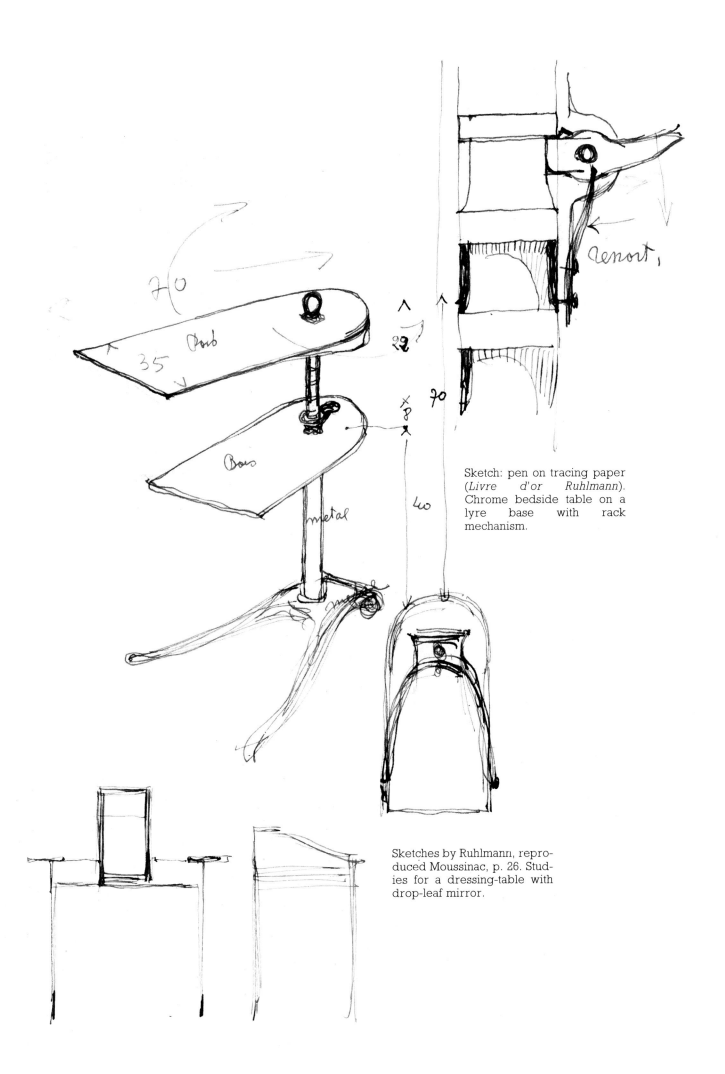

Sketch: pen on tracing paper (*Livre d'or Ruhlmann*). Chrome bedside table on a lyre base with rack mechanism.

Sketches by Ruhlmann, reproduced Moussinac, p. 26. Studies for a dressing-table with drop-leaf mirror.

Furniture designs. The vigorous and detailed sketches are in pen and ink, the proportions, the balance of mass and the fine details being transcribed with such accuracy that they seem to have been drawn from the finished piece. 'The idea for a piece of furniture takes shape as a whole in his mind. He immediately perceives its whole physiognomy. He conceives it as an organism whose character and life have to be captured.'

J. Laran, 'Enquête sur le mobilier moderne', *Art et Décoration*, January 1920.

In fashion houses, the stylist's design is always subject to interpretation, but Ruhlmann insisted that his ideas were to be scrupulously respected. His draughtsmen had to produce three sets of side and front elevations: a 1:100 drawing, a more detailed 1:10 plan and finally a full-scale working drawing for the cabinet-maker. At each stage, they referred back to the original sketch so as to remain faithful to the master's idea.[2] 'He would not have dreamed of using the old method of making a rough sketch of a decorative theme and then letting his foremen interpret it as they saw fit.'

G. Janneau, *Revue de l'art*, 1934, pp. 185ff.

He set the themes for the competitions he organized for his assistants on Saturdays, and he was the only judge. The author of the drawing chosen for the workshop's 'suggestion box' was congratulated and given a bonus, but the design was never executed in its original form. Ruhlmann invariably corrected it and left his own mark upon it.

In the thirties, in a comparative study entitled 'D'André-Charles Boulle à Ruhlmann', Guillaume Janneau, who was later to become *conservateur* of the Mobilier National, nostalgically invoked the important role played by *ancien régime* artisans, who left their personal mark on the furniture they produced. He likened Ruhlmann's working methods to those of the architects Percier and Fontaine who made the cabinet-makers of the Empire scrupulously follow designs that were perfect in every detail, reducing the craftsman to the status of a workman who simply followed orders. The comparison is somewhat exaggerated. The models of Percier and Fontaine are cold and meticulous, whereas Ruhlmann's sketches have a definite spontaneity. They are synthetic snapshots of his original inspiration and have a formal richness which he wanted his collaborators to respect. The originality of his working methods confirms the painter François Lemoyne's statement that 'It takes an artist twenty years to learn not to lose the qualities of his sketches.'

2 Sixty years later, Raymond Lautelin recalled that 'We could spend days or even weeks on a single study or a single detail. We had to start over and over again until we had achieved the desired effect. And then suddenly he would say, "Don't change anything! That's perfect!" He had an infallible eye and his decisions were final.'

Moussinac, pl. 17. Sketch, 1919
(Sketchbook 28)

Reuter table. Pen on tracing paper. *Livre d'or Ruhlmann.*

Should we regret the fact that Ruhlmann was not himself a cabinet-maker? An earlier commentator, Laran, justifies the absolute priority of the artist: 'The grammar of the professional is to be respected, but it is subordinate to imagination.'

Even when the full-scale drawing revealed technological difficulties, it was unusual for Ruhlmann to take out refinements he had introduced for their own sake, even if they would not be seen. He loved perfection *per se* and did not regard the bevelling of an unseen crosspiece as a superfluous detail. He refused to let his lack of practical knowledge stand in his way, and his interest in technical solutions shows how much he enjoyed being in the workshop. He brought Jules Deroubaix, who was one of his best cabinet-makers, over from the rue d'Ouessant, but not to act as a technical adviser: on the contrary, he did so in order to ensure that the work was carried out exactly according to his plans. 'Your craftsmanship is holding you back' was Ruhlmann's answer to every objection. Many years later, the unquestioningly loyal Deroubaix admitted that 'He was almost always right. He was a perfectionist, but he did not know how to work with his hands, so we had to innovate. He constantly challenged us to find adequate solutions.'

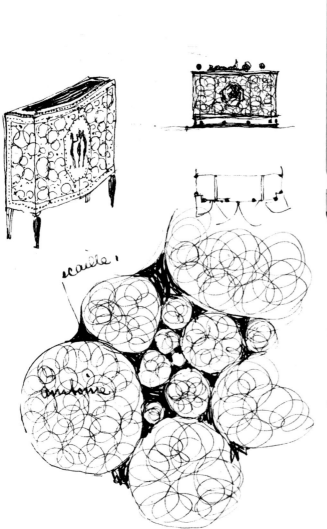

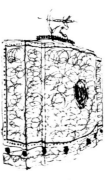

Elysée sideboard (see opposite). Design for marquetry in amboina-wood and ivory. Sketchbook 27, 1918. Sketch by Ruhlmann. Above: a smaller and simplified version made in 1927. The proportions have been somewhat modified (length: 160cm; height: 155cm). The bur amboina-wood veneer reduces the ivory to a narrow band, but the corners of the veneered pattern are marked by small squares of ivory. The position of the lock plate is marked by an octagonal inlay motif.

This page and overleaf
Elysée sideboard. Salon d'Automne, 1920. Probably the most remarkable piece of furniture ever made by Ruhlmann, both in terms of its dimensions (length: 329cm; Height: 186cm), its decoration (an irregular pattern of ivory and bur amboina-wood), the quality of the workmanship and its state of preservation. The octagonal lock plate in chased bronze (diameter:44cm) represents 'Day and Night' and is by Foucault. Acquired by the state in 1926 for the presidential Palais de l'Elysée and now in the Mobilier National. 'An exceptional piece of furniture, a true museum piece, which he showed with a certain pomp. A self-conscious masterpiece.' G Janneau, *Renaissance de l'art français*, January 1921.

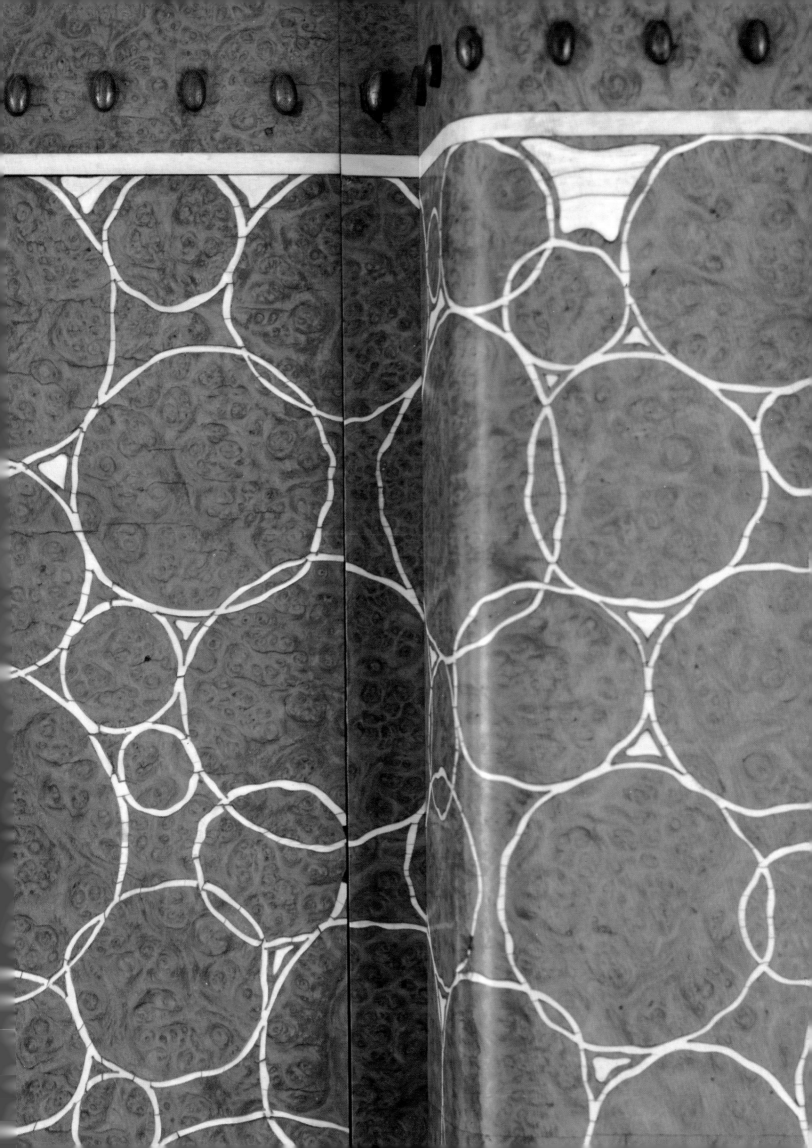

Sketches by Ruhlmann, reproduced Moussinac, pl.15.
Sketchbook 19, 1920.

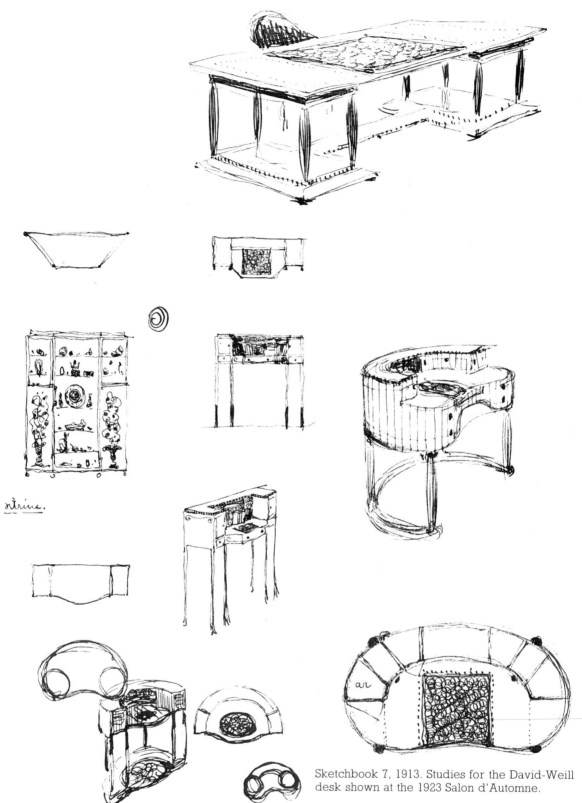

vitrine.

Sketchbook 7, 1913. Studies for the David-Weill
desk shown at the 1923 Salon d'Automne.

ELEMENTS OF STYLE

Architecture and geometry. All the interwar generation paid homage to architecture and regarded it as a normative discipline, but there were some differences of opinion as to its precise role. For the Bauhaus, architecture was a methodological guiding principle. For Pierre Patout, it was 'the cornerstone of the arts' and determined the structure, decoration and spatial arrangement of furniture. Maurice Dufrêne's statement that 'The furniture-designer is an architect' was authorized by Paul Valéry, whose character Eupalinos is an architect-geometer who materializes an ideal form of lines and volumes in furniture in the same way that the musician works with sounds.[3]

Les Arts décoratifs modernes, p. 75.

The designers of the twenties reacted against the curvilinear and naturalist fantasies of Art Nouveau by trying to circumscribe their contours in rigorous modules which place the emphasis on symmetry, stability and a purely rational simplicity. 'Behold the completely new sobriety of line in all the decorative arts!' exclaimed the architect Jean Badovici with enthusiasm. 'The soul of this geometry must have something to say to modern man.'

J. Badovici, *Intérieurs de Sue et Mare*, 1924.

The Triplan secretaire which Ruhlman exhibited at the 1913 Salon d'Automne, and which later gave rise to a number of variants, is a perfect example of this adaptation to a geometric structure: the front can be inscribed within an isosceles trapezium, and a section taken through the feet forms an irregular pentagon.

Some commentators have put forward the hypothesis that Ruhlmann was influenced by Cubism, and several sketches dating from 1913 seem to support this interpretation. In one, the square top of the table is connected to its conforming base either by a recessed cylindrical support or by four balls. In another, the square top and the octagonal base are linked by eight small columns. These sketches are not merely stylistic compositions, and the designs were executed (with some modifications); but this does not necessarily mean that Ruhlmann was inspired by Cubism. His decision to work in accordance with reason rather than whim represents an intellectual choice from which he never departed:

A. Frechet in *Mobiliers et décorations d'intérieur*, February–March 1924.

'An architectural drawing is a means and not an end.'

'Fine handwriting is not good literature.'

'Architecture is a celebration of common sense.'

3 Paul Valéry's essay on aesthetics, *Eupalinos ou l'architecte* (1927) was, it will be recalled, commissioned by the Compagnie des Arts Français.

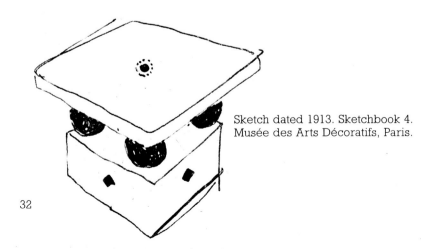

Sketch dated 1913. Sketchbook 4.
Musée des Arts Décoratifs, Paris.

petit crapaud

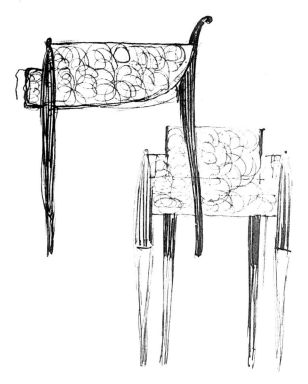

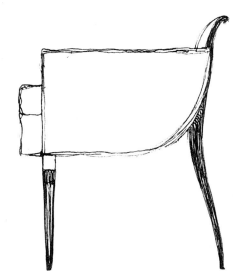

Studies for armchairs by Ruhlmann, reproduced by Moussinac, pl. 30. Sketchbook 27, 1918. Sketchbook 20, 1917. Sketchbook 20, 1917.

Overleaf
Three-leaf cheval-glass, *c.* 1920. Exhibited at the 1922 SAD. Ref. 1517 AR. Bur amboina-wood inlaid with ivory diamond pattern. Ivory dentil and volute on the ogee moulded base.

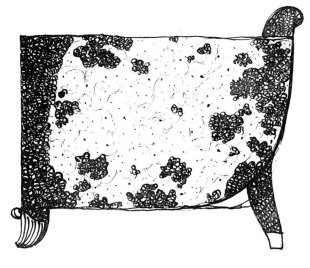

Rodier bar, 1930-31. Ref 1116 NR. Scroll base in
macassar ebony, lined with morocco, interior in
sycamore.

Triplan secretaire, 1923. Ref. 1530 AR/1609 NR. One of Ruhlmann's first pieces, shown at the 1913 Salon d'Automne.
According to the medallion, this example was made in 1923. Bur
amboina-wood, with five-sided legs tapering down to turned
feet. The two side doors fold down to form a writing platform.
All three sides are decorated with a diamond-shaped pattern in
ivory. Interior lined with grey morocco embossed with gold
pebbling.

These mottoes were coined to instil a sense of rigour into young draughtsmen, and they give some sense of Ruhlmann's clearsightedness and independence of mind. He subjected himself to an almost mathematical discipline and constantly altered the variants on a model in order to perfect the equilibrium of its mass and to ensure that the proportions were correct, working just like an architect or an engineer: 'He first ensured that his furniture produced an overall effect, and made people look at the whole rather than the details. Closer examination revealed delicate touches that only an expert could appreciate, the finer points and the beauty of the craftsmanship.'

G. Janneau, cited by H.V. Clouzot, *L'Illustration*, 28 June 1928.

Order and harmony. The decade 1919–29 marks a return to order, in both the moral and the architectural sense, in all areas of French artistic life. Traumatized by the war and by the collapse of values, many artists became convinced that an attachment to the nation's past was both an anchoring point and a springboard towards new certainties.

Was this a reactionary attitude? The avant-garde has no monopoly on truth. The modernists take credit for innovating and for sweeping away the past, but we also have to accept that others have every right to assert the continuity which unites different generations and which allows them to enrich the common patrimony.

In his *Propos sur l'art*, Matisse remarks that 'We are born with the sensibility of a particular period of civilization. Although they are so far apart and in many ways very different, Ingres and Delacroix begin to look similar if we look at their work from a distance.' The comparison becomes even more meaningful when applied to Ruhlmann and Le Corbusier or Chareau. Ruhlmann aimed at harmony, Le Corbusier and Chareau at ascetic rigour, but they all share the view that 'Order is a sign of man's mastery of matter.'

J. Badovici, '*Harmonies.*' *Intérieurs de Ruhlmann, 1913–1924*, Paris 1924.

In his attempt to produce sophisticated harmonies, Ruhlmann used fluting to bring to life the front of a commode or the sides of cigar boxes in silvered metal. This was no mere stylistic cliché, and the same rigour can be seen in his designs for chair-legs, lamps and silver-cabinets.

He delighted in making comments about the pieces sent to the Salon des Artistes Décorateurs by his competitors. One of his former collaborators recalls his double-edged remark about the stand of the Compagnie des Arts Français: 'It is extremely well made. But it is a bit fat,' he said, pointing to a line that was too rounded, an upright that was too curved. He himself constantly reworked his full-scale drawings to introduce yet more sobriety and refinement. For critics, Ruhlmann's sense of discipline was the mark of his superiority.

J. Badovici, op. cit.

'In furniture design, achieving simplicity is the most difficult art of all. It takes uncommon skill and an incomparable sureness of taste to mould these almost imperceptible curves, to choose the one curve that will give the piece its ''character'' and its supreme elegance.' Ruhlmann's favourite line was that of the ogee, a double curved moulding, concave above and convex below. Its movement is at once harmonious, gentle and mathematically precise. Ruhlmann used it for bases (the Colonnettes dressing-table), pediments (the Nicolle drinks cabinet) and even for the underside of pedestal tables – an apparently superfluous refinement, as it could not be seen. The barely perceptible 'movement which shifts the lines' fades into the flat surfaces; trims of ivory or silvered metal give them their rhythm. The whole art of the stylist lies in the composition and distribution of planes and volumes.

Tradition and classicism. Ruhlmann was without doubt the most prolific furniture-designer of the twentieth century, if not in the entire history of French furniture. He was self-taught and worked as an amateur before turning professional. He had no formal training at the Ecole Boulle or the Ecole des Arts Décoratifs to predispose him to look for inspiration in the past, and he was thirty-four when he exhibited for the first time.

Disconcerted by the novelty of his aesthetic, commentators suspected him of being inspired by the Munich Werkbund school, as though the rejection of complicated forms in favour of simple planes and volumes was a national characteristic.

Being the son of an Alsatian who had sided with France, Ruhlmann could not be suspected of being either a German sympathizer or a French chauvinist. When Pascal Forthuny organized a poll on the advisability of inviting the Germans to the 1925 Exposition Internationale des Arts Décoratifs, Ruhlmann was 'one of those who wanted a fight. . . Our industrialists have a lot to learn from these formidable competitors, whose discipline is so strict and so fertile, whose sense of organization is so perfect. . . Struggle is stimulating and educational, and even if it does lead to temporary reverses, it is preferable to sleep. I am for the struggle. Let them come.'

L'Amour de l'art, 1922, pp. 61–62.

Ruhlmann felt no need to disown his illustrious forebears. He obviously felt a certain affinity with the period that produced the Louis XVI, Directoire, Empire and Restoration styles, and it is not impossible that some of his pieces might derive from earlier models. His personal taste was that of an educated bourgeois, and he wanted to reconcile tradition and modernity. For his bourgeois clients he updated pieces whose typology evokes a somewhat dated art of living: *causeuses*, silver-

Make-up cabinet, *c*. 1930. Ref 2302 NR. The original model shown in 1927 had a stepped base and a fluted vertical pedestal. This variant in American bur walnut shows the results of formal research designed to emphasize the volume. The decoration has been reduced to a chased octagonal lock plate in silvered bronze by Foucault.

Fluted chiffonier. 1927–28. Ref. 2043 AR/2303 NR. An imposing pedestal piece in bur amboina-wood with a half-moon front. The broad fluting gives the piece its rhythm, the only relief on the doors being provided by the chased octagonal lock plate by Janniot.

cabinets, *bonheurs-du-jour* and chiffoniers all have connotations of refinement that are far removed from Le Corbusier's irreverent pragmatism: 'You sit on them, work on them, use them, wear them out and then replace them.'

Even when the prototypes for certain pieces – such as the *méridienne* and the day-bed – belong to a particular period, Ruhlmann does not approach them in a spirit of parody or plagiarism. His free interpretations were inspired by the prototypes, but they always took into account the requirements of comfort and originality. They all bear the mark of his individual talent (for example, the Hanck and Bienvenu divans in wood and the couches in marble or Comblanchien limestone). The *chaise-gondole* also inspired variations which give it a completely new look, like the Tauzin chair, in which the back is reduced to a mere suggestion of a curve.

There are, however, specific examples in which Ruhlmann seems deliberately to have learned from the past: thus, he went back to the Empire style for the dignified chairs in the salon in the Hôtel du Collectionneur (the prototype was known as the Fontainebleau chair). At first sight, the flat Ambassade 1925 desk, designed for a French Embassy, looks like a conventional pedestal desk (a large number were ordered). But closer examination reveals a classically Ruhlmann touch: an imperceptible curve relieves the flatness of the rectangular top and the legs are outlined by an ivory trim running down to the *sabot*.

Rather than accusing the designer of conformism, we should perhaps remember that aristocratic prejudices still survive. The two-tiered kidney-shaped desk made for David-Weill (a famous connoisseur of antique furniture) typifies both Ruhlmann's intuitive understanding of period style and his creativity. He seizes the opportunity to prove that he can satisfy the most rigorous technological demands.

Mention might also be made of the Tibattant lady's secretaire and the roll-top desk, whose proportions and harmonious construction are worthy of a Louis XVI cabinet-maker. Such stylistic compositions suggest that Ruhlmann was a classicist whose aim was to transcend fashion and to arrive at a timeless style, but the references to the past are a mark of respect and not a sign of his inability to find a style of his own. Indeed, furniture-designers and critics unanimously hailed him as the 'Riesener of the twentieth century'.

The role of decoration. Ruhlmann belonged to a generation which rejected the naturalistic Art Nouveau fantasies of the Ecole de Nancy. Without totally renouncing the attractions of floral decoration, they

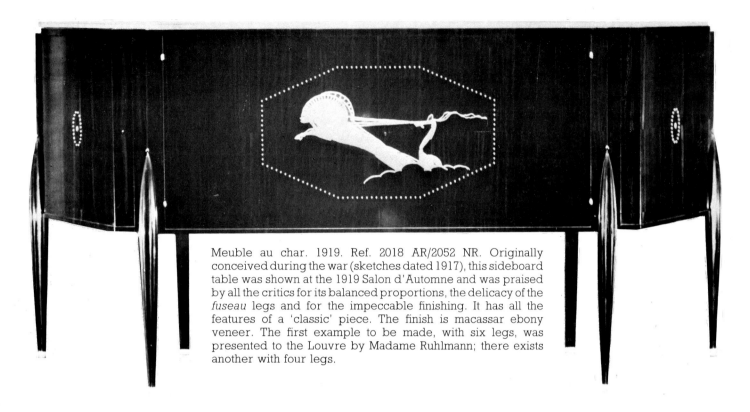

Meuble au char. 1919. Ref. 2018 AR/2052 NR. Originally conceived during the war (sketches dated 1917), this sideboard table was shown at the 1919 Salon d'Automne and was praised by all the critics for its balanced proportions, the delicacy of the *fuseau* legs and for the impeccable finishing. It has all the features of a 'classic' piece. The finish is macassar ebony veneer. The first example to be made, with six legs, was presented to the Louvre by Madame Ruhlmann; there exists another with four legs.

Above and overleaf
David-Weill kidney-shaped desk. Ref. 1516 AR/1520a NR. Salon d'Automne, 1923. Made for the antique collector David-Weill. Ruhlmann modified a single-tier desk originally designed in 1918–19 for the dress-designer Fernande Cabanel. The small curved tier contains miniature drawers and pigeon-holes. The delicately rounded sections on either side of the central drawer both contain drawers. The shagreen writing pad and the *fuseau* legs give the piece a distinction unequalled since the eighteenth century.

Overleaf
Roll-top desk. Ref. 1512 AR/1603 NR. Salon des Artistes Décorateurs, 1923. Macassar ebony, interior in amboina-wood, writing pad in shagreen and ivory. The curved front legs taper down to minuscule ivory *sabots* which follow the line of the carved trim which emphasizes the curve of the legs. The edge of the roll top is picked out with ivory and ebony dentils.

subjected it to a more or less realistic stylization until about 1925, at which point they began to be influenced by Cubism. At the 1927 Salon des Artistes Décorateurs, Léon Werth was struck by the new emphasis on geometrical ornament, which he rightly saw as 'a compromise between the need for decoration and the outdated means whereby that need could be fulfilled. Whereas the arbitrary use of a rose would be intolerable, the arbitrary use of a triangle or a sphere gives an illusion of rigour and necessity. A caprice can be disguised as geometry.'

'Le XVIIᵉ Salon des Artistes Décorateurs', *Art et Décoration*, June 1927.

Relief. Although he was not especially interested in ornamentation, in the early stages of his career Ruhlmann did occasionally give in to the temptation to use carving and marquetry as figurative decoration. Only a few examples of each type can be mentioned here, but they are all spectacular pieces. One of the variations on the *demi-ventre* silver-cabinet features a basket of flowers in pure Art Déco style, whilst the composition of the '*coffret or* with *fuseau* legs' and the Ducharne desk is, to say the least, unexpected.

After 1920, the decorator stopped using carved motifs, as they were incompatible with his flat veneered surfaces. He replaced them with repeated motifs such as ribbing, fluting and juxtaposed beadings. The three doors of the Geoffroy silver-cabinet feature a square motif of concentric beading which is proportional to the cubic volume of the base and the cupboards.

The chased plaques which mask the locks and the join between the doors, and whose role is ornamental rather than functional, can be regarded as sculpted decorations. In pieces veneered with amboina-wood, the bronze is silvered; when darker woods such as macassar ebony or American bur walnut are used, it may be either silvered or gilded. The bronzes are by two winners of the Grand Prix de Rome, whose sculptures were exhibited in his premises in the rue de Lisbonne, and they are remarkable in terms of both their format and their allegorical composition.[4]

Most Ruhlmann silver-cabinets have lock plates using a variety of formats and motifs. The lock plate by the Martel brothers is of particular interest in that its Cubist inspiration represents a departure from the usual style of the Ruhlmann group.

4 Foucault created an octagonal openwork motif with a 'day and night' theme for the 'Elysée' sideboard. Several years later, it was used again for the 'Ducharne' silver-cabinet. Two different plaques were used for the make-up cabinet at different times. The first, a woman holding draperies, was chased by Foucault, and was later used for the fluted chiffonier. The second, a dancing nymph seen in profile, was by Janniot.

Solid furniture is dominated by the visible architecture of the uprights and crosspieces, but in laminated Art Déco furniture the frame is concealed. Daring use can therefore be made of facings, and carved or appliqué reliefs play a relatively minor role. An Art Déco piece 'gives the impression of being a monolith carved out in one piece. There are no visible supports and its imposing bulk seems to float in space. There are no frames and no relief mouldings. There are no projecting parts; everything is flush. The tops of these pieces are stepped back, like plinths, rather than overhanging.'

Art et décoration,
January 1927.

Marquetry: ivory and tortoiseshell. Always sensitive to contrasts of material and colour, Ruhlmann favoured cabinet-making techniques which integrate ornamentation and veneering. Grains dyed in different colours, burs and other natural excrescences found in wood provided natural decorative motifs, and his cabinet-makers used them to produce a variety of optical effects: contrasting squares of American bur walnut with broad concentric whorls; violet-wood cut into narrow horizontal beading hinting at the unseen curved verticals; slats of macassar ebony which, when a roll-top desk was closed, formed a continuous pattern and looked like a section cut through the wood itself.

Until 1925, Ruhlmann was not content with exploiting the natural resources of these exotic woods. He heightened the effect by inlaying them with strings or pearls of ivory forming sunburst or geometric patterns ('sun' veneer, squares, rectangles, diamonds). This technique allowed him to emphasize the curve of a vertical or a leg, to conceal doors and drawers beneath ivory latticework and to decorate pediments, bases and backs with spirals, dentils and regular wave patterns. All these subtle details justify Ruhlmann's own description of these finely worked pieces as 'precious'.

In a few exceptional cases, ivory was used for marquetry, the work being done by outside ivory carvers who worked on commission from cartoons. On two occasions, Ruhlmann used figurative designs. The bur amboina-wood corner cupboard made in 1916 has a distinctive large medallion in ivory and ebony representing a vase of flowers. The *Meuble au Char* takes its name from the discreet and stylized inlaid classical chariot motif by Pico. The *Meuble au Char* is unique in the history of furniture-making. Three of its sides are veneered with an ivory lattice; the individual units of the irregular mesh are inlaid with amboina-wood. A sketch reproduced by Moussinac suggests that the artist initially intended to use tortoiseshell. When used in combination with ebony or shagreen, the ivory pebbling on the top of a dressing-table becomes

Etat d'angle, 1916. Ref. 1521 AR/2233 NR. Corner cupboard with a *bombé* front decorated with a vase of flowers in ivory and ebony marquetry – the only example of this motif in Ruhlmann's *oeuvre*. The piece acquired by the state in 1922 is in amaranth; the one shown here in bur amboina-wood.

Opposite
Frieze of a chiffonier in amboina-wood, *c.* 1922–23. Ref. 1513 AR/2235 NR. The close-up photograph brings out the architectural effect of the ornamentation. The volute and the palmette motifs gently but firmly emphasize the strict but pleasing lines of this chiffonier.

trompe-l'oeil embroidery which covers part of the front and conceals the drawer.

In the years that followed the 1925 Exposition des Arts Décoratifs, Ruhlmann used less ivory, even on lock surrounds and drawer handles, replacing it with silver-chrome bronze, which he thought more appropriate to the sober, bare lines of his later style.

Although he rarely used tortoiseshell, Ruhlmann did sometimes use it as a veneer, dying it red or green to improve the sheen. The Nicolle drinks cabinet is inlaid with tortoiseshell and ivory fillets, the Schueller secretaire with tortoiseshell and bronze.

Shagreen and lacquer. Paradoxically, these techniques, which are specific to Art Déco which mastered them and adapted them to furniture with a remarkable degree of success, were rarely used by Ruhlmann. He saw himself as working in the tradition of the great cabinet-makers and was reluctant to draw attention away from wood, that most noble and traditional of materials.

Shagreen is the regularly grained skin of a ray found in the south seas. In the eighteenth century it was used for covering small objects. Working it is a delicate and costly process which produces a pale or milky white satin-like surface, a specialist skill handed down in secret from craftsman to craftsman and which has more in common with leatherwork than with cabinet-making. Ruhlmann used shagreen with discretion, sometimes together with ivory, and restricted it to specific areas such as the tops of tables and desks, which would normally be covered in leather or doeskin. Examples of this technique include desk and table tops pebbled with ivory and shagreen, the sunburst veneers of the Ambassade 1925 desk, which was probably made by Chanaux in his own workshops, and the Maréchal Lyautey desk in the Musée des Colonies.[5] In later years, shagreen was used only for specially commissioned pieces. The dressing-table shown in the 1928 'state' bedroom (*chambre d'apparat*) is covered in snakeskin, and the last lady's desk shown in 1933 is covered entirely in morocco.[6]

Ruhlmann made few lacquered pieces, as the exceptional decorative qualities of lacquer detracted from the cabinet-work itself. They were made in collaboration with Jean Dunand. In 1925, Dunand decorated the central doors of a large sideboard for the Hôtel du Collectionneur (see

5 A comparison can usefully be drawn between Groult and Ruhlmann, both of whom created a *lit-corbeille* which has survived. Groult used shagreen for his extraordinary Embassy bedroom. In 1928 Ruhlmann exhibited a model with triple veneering in bur amboina-wood. The *ébénisterie* alone took 1200 hours of work, not to mention the satin upholstery.
6 Now in the Musée des Arts Décoratifs.

p. 88), working from a maquette by Jean Lambert-Rucki.[7] Working with the same materials, Dunand created an asymmetrical harmony in black and silver for the dressing-table exhibited by Ruhlmann at the 1927 Salon des Artistes Décorateurs.

Shortly after this, Ruhlmann set up a workshop for lacquer-spraying (a process similar to the use of cellulose paint) in his premises in the rue d'Ouessant. Duco lacquer offers limited artistic possibilities; but, being waterproof, tough, neutral and economical, it has its purely functional role. Ruhlmann restricted it to plain furniture with astonishingly modern lines.

He adopted it for the Tardieu desk and for the modular bookcase shown at the 1929 Salon des Artistes Décorateurs. These late pieces, whose beauty lies in the purity of the proportions, the clean lines and the monochrome, are far removed from the 'Byzantine complications' denounced by Le Corbusier.

7 When the piece shown in Barcelona was sold in 1928, Dunand added two other doors decorated with a silver lacquered geometrical composition on a black ground. This Cubist picture was in accordance with the buyer's tastes. Lambert-Rucki's composition *Donkey and Hedgehog* was later mounted separately as a decorative panel.

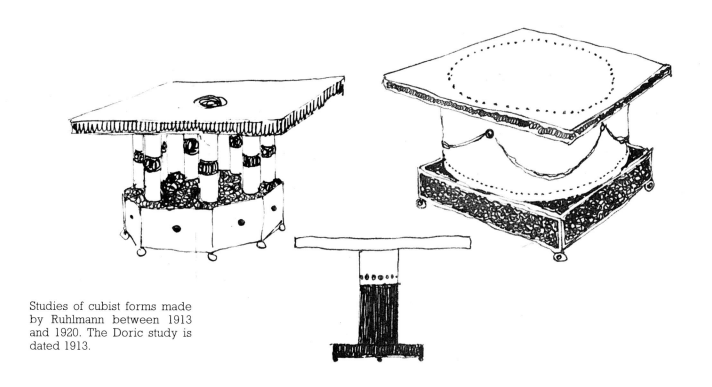

Studies of cubist forms made by Ruhlmann between 1913 and 1920. The Doric study is dated 1913.

Legs and bases. Ruhlmann's creativity found expression not only in the architecture and ornamentation of his furniture, but also in his refusal to remain trapped by a successful stylistic formula. This is one way of interpreting his various approaches to the problem of the support.

Until 1916, he opted for a classic support: the typically Louis XVI square, tapering leg. But even before the end of the war Ruhlmann had attracted the attention of both critics and rivals by introducing an innovatory modification. The feet were no longer placed beneath his chairs and tables, but at a slight angle to them: they no longer supported them but propped them up effortlessly. The effect of attaching the legs half way up a piece of furniture is to increase its height and to create the impression of a fragile construction which centres upon the tiny volute which marks the joint. Although it is impossible to see precisely where the leg joins the frame, the solidity and credibility of the piece are never in doubt. Each leg is carved out of the carcase and veneered separately to draw attention to it (this sophisticated technique meant that it took a week to make each leg).

Ruhlmann's *fuseau* leg is unique. It had its critics, but also its admirers and imitators. It is the unmistakable mark of a Ruhlmann piece, and it still comes as a surprise to see that it can support a piece as heavy as the *Meuble au Char*. Ruhlmann also used the *fuseau* leg on armchairs. Although these are light, they give the impression that the weight is carried by the feet, whereas it is the construction of the legs and the seat which is crucial.

There are two types of *fuseau* leg: the *fuselé cannelé* (see p. 57) and the *fuselé à facettes* (see p. 69). The former has eight flutings and its almost disconcerting slenderness is accentuated by the tall ivory *sabot*. The *fuselé à facettes* is less graceful, but the ivory-inlaid edges are impeccably designed.

From 1923 onwards, the angled *fuseau* leg was replaced by a prismatic leg which follows the line of the sides but is no longer a separate element. This variation was used for large pieces like the Fontane and Cabanel chiffoniers.

The gradual move away from the *fuseau* leg, which confined Ruhlmann to a precious style, marked the appearance of the transitional curved leg. The only thing the two have in common is that they are both set at a slight angle. (The Ambassade 1925 desk is the prototype.) The affected slenderness thus gave way to a classical sobriety which defies changes in fashion. When the actress Jeanne Renouardt commissioned a dressing-table shown in the Hôtel du Collectionneur in 1930, Ruhlmann replaced the *fuseau* legs with gently curving vertical legs.

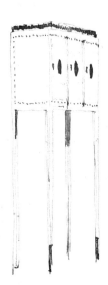

Rothschild *bonheur-du-jour*. Ref. 1523 AR/2201 NR. Circa 1920. Sketch by Ruhlmann.

Ruhlmann was simultaneously experimenting with an equally novel base that was the complete antithesis of the *fuseau* legs which supported these tall pieces. He designed two cabinets in amboina-wood inlaid with ivory which stood on the floor or, to be more accurate, on a carpeted dais.[8]

In most cases, an empty space broken by fluted balls in silver bronze separates the piece from its base. This arrangement gives a feeling of rhythm and ensures that the volume is displayed to maximum advantage. Examples include the monumental Elysée sideboard and the Ducharne and Worms silver-cabinets, in which the base has the same lines as the arched doors. The Geoffroy cabinet, in contrast, is supported by a recessed ogee base with three chromium-plated motifs in the round. Variants include pieces on fluted runners, ribbed scrolls or ogee bases. In all cases, the desired effect is to avoid banality and to ensure that the piece rests lightly on the floor.

8 The carpeted dais was used for display purposes in exhibitions. Ruhlmann recommended it to collectors as a safety precaution rather than for reasons of ostentation.

Lotus dressing-table, 1919; Wood and metal dressing-table, 1929. These dressing-tables are separated by an interval of only ten years, but it is difficult to imagine them as being by the same designer.

In his last years, Ruhlmann used two types of base, one functional and the other decorative. The former conceals storage boxes with invisible locks and handles. In the latter an upright which miraculously supports the entire weight is set into a slender recessed ogee moulding. The 'make-up cabinet' (*Meuble à fards*) and the fluted chiffonier were both constructed in accordance with this principle and are rightly described as ceremonial pieces (*meubles d'apparat*).

From traditional ébénisterie to new materials. Strongly marked by the machine civilization produced by the war, the twenties represent a transitional period in which non-conventional materials like metal and glass began to challenge techniques hallowed by centuries of use. As Léon Werth noted in 1927, 'We live in an age of metal. We want our furniture to be as streamlined as carriagework. Whether we like it or not, the forms of the car and the aeroplane are acting upon our visual sensibilities and transforming them.'

L. Werth, 'Le XVIIᵉ Salon des Artistes Décorateurs', *Art et décoration*, June 1927.

Creative artists experienced this change in a variety of ways. In both Germany and France, the avant-garde rejected the furniture of the past and looked for purely functional models. The neo-classicists were more strongly attached to the *ébénisterie* tradition and found it more difficult to accept the change, particularly as they had taken laminating techniques to new heights of perfection.

By using these techniques skilfully and carefully cabinet-makers could prevent wood from being warped by variations in temperature and humidity.[9] The same cannot be said of the masterpieces of Boulle and Oeben, in which the marquetry or veneer is applied direct to only one side of the wood. Construction methods could not be altered to any great extent unless, using materials other than wood, a completely new technology was applied. . . and that meant the death of *ébénisterie*. This was not, however, Ruhlmann's intention when in 1918 he used the principles of joinery to design an assemblage of wood and metal.[10] He was simply trying to overcome the harmful effects of central heating.[11]

9 Experiments with lamination were carried out in the mid-nineteenth century, but it was twentieth-century cabinet-makers who mastered the art. Wood does not warp along the line of the grain. Narrow strips of wood are glued at right angles to the grain on either side of a core panel (known as the *âme* or soul), to cancel out the movement. Ruhlmann used Hungarian oak laminated with tulipwood, which is absolutely stable, and then applied the precious veneers lengthways on both faces of the *âme*. In solid, as distinct from laminated, furniture the panels and the flexible verticals which hold them together are arranged in such a way as to counteract the warp.
10 A description and diagram of the construction method, which Ruhlmann intended to patent, can be found in Sketchbook 28 (1918), pp. 31 *bis*, 32.
11 He told Léon Deshairs that in the USA central heating at 72°F (22°C) made old veneers crumble into dust. 'If we want to export our furniture to that country, where it is appreciated, it has to be robust as well as beautiful.' Cited, 'Une Etape vers le meuble métallique', *Art et décoration*, 1927.

At the 1926 Salon des Artistes Décorateurs, Ruhlmann exhibited a study – desk and bookcase – designed in accordance with traditional joinery techniques, except that the sliding solid wood panels were set in metal grooves. If we compare these semi-metallic pieces with the desk shown that year by Pierre Chareau, the contrast between the neo-classicists and the modernists becomes obvious: refinement as opposed to austere simplicity, harmonious proportions as opposed to cold angularity, finely worked metal as opposed to machined wrought iron.[12]

The following year, Ruhlmann took his experiment further still with a sheet-metal bookcase made according to his design by Raymond Subes. Only one such bookcase was made, and it was described by a critic as a perfect example of 'furniture designed for a mechanical civilization and a deforested universe'. Ruhlmann could not, however, reconcile himself to the raw look of the metal: the structures may well have a metallic sheen, but the patina of the lacquered doors looks ambiguously like a more noble material.

It would be unfair to hold this against a creator who was in many respects a pioneer. It should not be forgotten that until 1930 metal furniture was still in its infancy and that it seemed unlikely that it would soon be competing with traditional furniture, at least not in the domestic sphere. In theory, metal furniture was designed for mass production; in practice it was regarded as a prototype and was sold to collectors at prohibitive prices. Ruhlmann's experiments represented a realistic option on the future. His experiments produced two small occasional tables. One had a lyre base and was supported by a collapsible support in chromium-plated steel; the other combined wood and metal and lent itself to a wide range of uses.

Ruhlmann's building and decorating business helped him to appreciate the decorative and functional qualities of industrial glass; after all, he did employ thirty-five mirror cutters on a permanent basis. Comments reported by Maximilien Gauthier make one regret that his premature death prevented this great pioneer from realizing his ambitions. 'This totally incomparable material opens up whole new horizons! It is translucent and incorruptible. It can be burnished or frosted and can be worked in all sorts of ways. It can be ground or sand-blasted. It can be gilded or silvered, used flat or moulded to any curve. There is enough here to make artists and scientists dream and experiment for ever.'[13]

12 The entire silvered steel structure slots together and is held in place by exposed screws. The top and sides are in richly veined macassar ebony. The fluted tubes project at an angle and support the table without drawing attention to their function.
13 Cited, *Art vivant*, October 1934. Unfortunately, the comments are not dated with any precision. Gauthier merely states that Ruhlmann made them shortly before his death in response to a questionnaire, but there is no reason to doubt their veracity.

Ruhlmann respected the past, but he was also capable of looking into the future and mastering it. 'Glass furniture! What an unhoped-for future!' Putting his new ideas into practice, in 1929 he produced a prototype dressing-table (p. 51) in which he proved that wood, metal and sheets of glass could complement one another.[14] It is difficult to believe that this futuristic creation was made only ten years after the lotus-base dressing-table in ivory and ebony marquetry, the perfect symbol of the art of *ébénisterie*.

Cited by M.A. Dayot, *Les Arts et les artistes*, January 1935.

Although a tenacious legend persists that Ruhlmann was the most brilliant representative of traditionalism, he himself summed up his programme in just three words: 'Rationalism, comfort, progress.' He foresaw that furniture would develop along the same lines as ships, railway carriages and aeroplanes, all of which had originally been made of wood: 'Furniture will be made from metal,' he prophesied. 'It will be finished in impeccable and incombustible lacquer.'

Ruhlmann modernized the precious aesthetics of the pedestal table, replacing the carved wooden pedestal with two planished metal lyres. He even studied the spray-painted sheet-metal fittings used in officers' cabins on warships.

Dayot, op. cit.

He believed that evolution has to take account of new realities: 'We have to translate the beauty of pure, rational form into fine materials. . . We often see poor, rebarbative machine-made pieces masquerading as rationalism, and it has to be said that they are aesthetically indigestible. But there is no denying that there is something attractive about contemporary experiments, or that studying them has its charms. It is obvious to any informed observer that there can be no going back.'

According to Eugène Ionesco, there is no antithesis between the avant-garde and classicism, because any true creator is a classicist. His comment applies perfectly to Ruhlmann, whose career was summed up by Claude Roger-Marx as 'Twenty years of detailed research governed by a desire for perfection, by an aristocratic taste and by absolute resistance to the extravagances and pendulum swings of fashion'.

'La Rétrospective Ruhlmann', *Europe nouvelle*, 3 November 1934.

We have to do away with the myth of a pioneering creator who became trapped by the style he established and with which posterity identifies him: 'Ruhlmann's mind was so subtle and so receptive to contemporary developments that he would certainly have evolved greatly over the last fifteen years had not his premature death removed him from the contemporary art world. It has to be said that while those who continue his work may have been inspired by the work he actually produced, they can give us no idea of the work he might have produced had he but lived.'

Art présent, 1947.

14 Two delightful uprights in veneered violet-wood linked by a chromium-plated base support a large kidney-shaped sheet of glass. The effect is completed by three metal-framed mirrors. The legs are also metal. (See p. 51.)

Ducharne bar. 1930. Display and storage unit standing against the wall. The fluted façade forms an arc of a circle. The feet and braces of the high stools are chromium-plated, as is the foot rail. Copies were made in both macassar ebony and in Duco lacquer finish.

Bar on skis, 1930. Ref. 2223 NR. A lacquered and fluted drinks cabinet mounted upon chromium-plated skis to form a mobile bar. Also made in macassar ebony.

Sketches made by Ruhlmann during the 1914–18
war. Reproduced, Moussinac, pl. 33. Sketchbook
11, 1915; Sketchbook 20, 1917. Sketchbook 11,
1915.

Nicolle drinks cabinet, 1926. Ref 1543 AR. A precious *entre-deux* cabinet in macassar ebony standing on ribbed *fuseau* legs. The doors are veneered with squares of tortoiseshell and are surrounded by an ivory dentil. Recessed top on an ogee moulded pediment. The lock plate is the only indication of the invisible join between the doors.

Overleaf: Fontacharne chiffonier, 1926. Ref. 1516 AR/2234 NR. Rosewood. The pronounced curve of the front legs is mid way between the line of the *fuseau* leg and that of the transitional leg. Lock plate in silver-chrome bronze by the Martel brothers.
Overleaf right: detail of p. 38.

Chinoise dressing-table. Salon des Artistes Décorateurs, 1927. Ref. 1538 AR/1827 NR. A simple solid form whose beauty lies in the use of eggshell lacquer on a black background. Abstract design by Jean Dunand. The chair is also lacquered. The front legs are known as 'tusks' (*défenses*) because of their tapering line. A unique piece purchased by Miss Redhead for 18,900 francs. Collection of Michael Chow.

Opposite: Cabanel chiffonier. Circa 1921-22. Ref. 2232 NR. The slender legs form part of the frame and are placed close together to suggest the delicacy of the construction. The ivory diamond pattern brings out the warm marbling of the macassar ebony without concealing the doors. White silk cords were originally attached to the door handles.

Collectionneur desk. 1925. Ref. 1063 AR/1541 NR. The fluted five-sided leg is set at a slight angle and forms part of the frame. Legs carved and then veneered with American bur walnut. The recessed top is edged with ivory beading.

Schueller silver-cabinet. 1928. Ref. 1550 AR/2230 NR. The close-up shows the juxtaposition of the continuous frieze of semi-circular beading in solid timber and the plain, diamond-patterned veneer of the doors.

Hanck divan. 1922. Ref. 527 AR/508 NR. A classic day-bed or *canapé*, but there is no question of lack of inspiration on the part of the designer. Definitely reminiscent of the early nineteenth century, but the refinement of the ivory ornaments which follow the rising curve of the base and symmetrically break up the precious veneers makes it a distinctively Ruhlmann piece. This divan was shown in the salon of the Hôtel du Collectionneur in 1925. Examples were made in rosewood, macassar ebony and amboina-wood. Galerie Lesieutre.

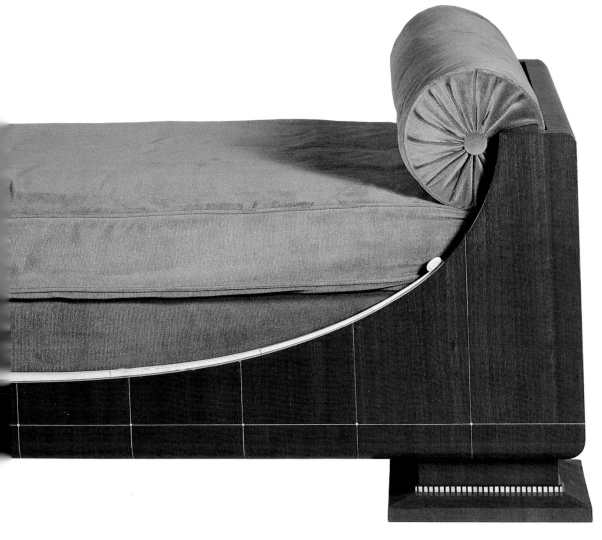

Spirales Divan. 1920–22. Ref. 532 AR/518 Nr. Bur amboina-wood with ivory pearls. The unusually elegant spiral motif on the side immediately marks this bed as a Ruhlmann piece. The prototype had sloping headrests. Galerie Lesieutre.

Colonnettes dressing-table. 1918–19. Ref. 1508 AR. Macassar ebony with ivory fillets, dentils and pearls. The ivory and shagreen marquetry of the central trim or tapis extends down over the front. The semicircular top is supported at the front by two turned columns with octagonal capitals and at the back by a stele surmounted by a swing glass. The ogee profile of the base counter-balances the light horizontals and verticals of the frame.

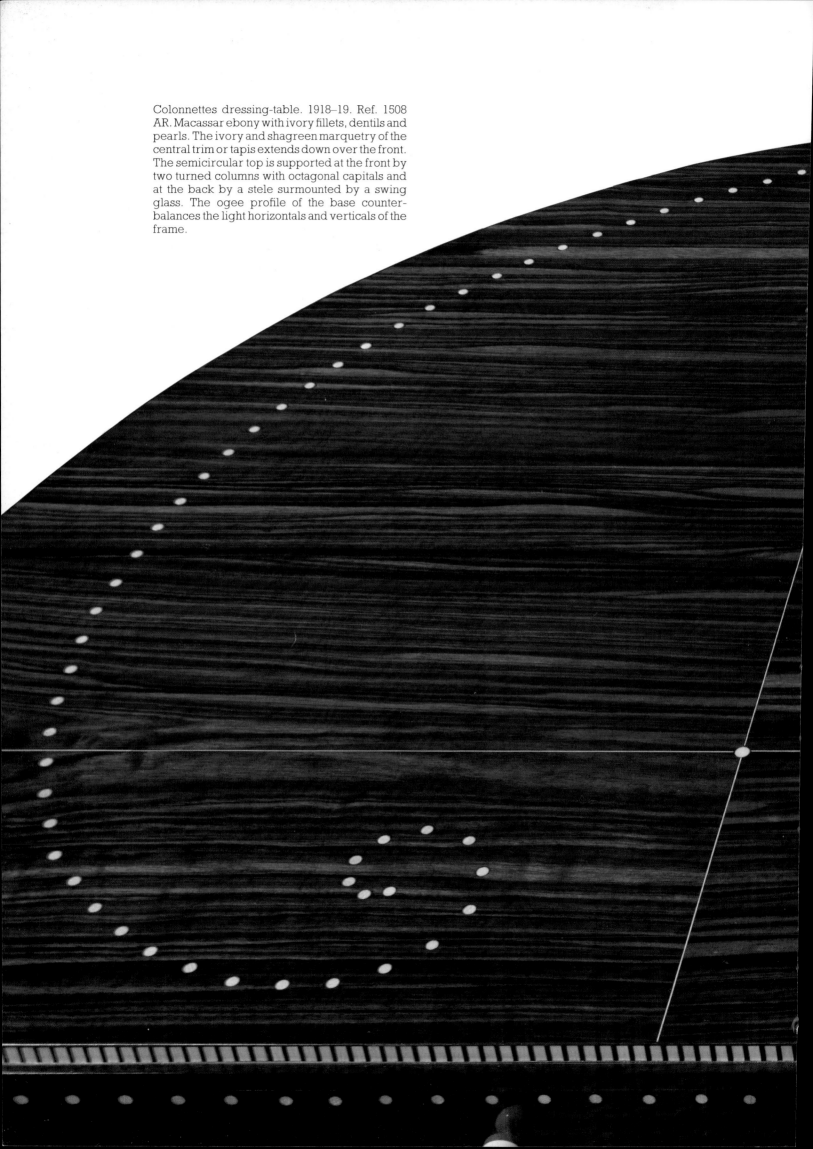

Fuseau cabinet. 1926. A variation on the Nicolle cabinet. An ivory dentil outlines the doors, which are veneered in red tortoiseshell and inlaid with an unbroken diamond pattern in ivory.

Preceding pages: Collectionneur dressing-table. Martelet variation. Circa 1928. Ref. 1822a NR. Bur amboina-wood veneer, top inlaid with shagreen and ivory. The squat legs taper down like billiard cues to the ivory sabots.

Faceted Fuseau leg in bur amboina-wood. The close-up shows the joint marked by the ivory bead and allows us to appreciate the extraordinary precision of the veneered facets and the ivory inlays on their edges.

Overleaf
Meuble au Char. Detail. The classical motif of a chariot driven by a slender figure is by Pico, a young collaborator of Ruhlmann's. The idea for it came from Ruhlmann himself. The octagonal ivory border, a solid fillet here, is a dotted line in the original version. The stylized motif, based on the antique, plays on contrasts of colour and material.

71

Lambiotte occasional table. 1929. Ref. 1257a NR. A variation on the Lambiotte fire-screen, which has a vertically tilting top. Examples were made in bur amboina-wood and in American bur walnut. This small table has a fixed top and is, if we examine it in detail, a masterpiece of cabinet-making. Galerie Lesieutre, formerly in the collection of Ruhlmann's doctor, Dr Rabaud.

Overleaf
Tardieu desk. Salon des Artistes Décorateurs, 1929. Ref. 1511 NR. The prototype, purchased by the French prime minister, André Tardieu, was, like that of the modular bookcase, in black lacquer, but was already intended for the Maharajah of Indore, all of whose office furniture was in macassar ebony. The semicircular positioning of the pigeonholes and the telephone, wastepaper basket and bellpush is extremely functional. The carefully contrived contrast between the wood and chromium-plated metal is to be noted. The unusual chairs, with the single rear leg broadening out to form the back, were in fact made for a games table.

Japonaise table. 1918–20. Ref. 1005 AR/1112 NR. Precious in detail and architectural in design, this little table has a concealed drawer in the centre. Discreet use of ivory pearls and beading. Others were made in amaranth, bur amboina-wood, American bur walnut, rosewood and lacquered oak. Galerie Valoise.

Maharajah of Indore modular bookcase. Macassar ebony. The bookcase consists of modules which can be juxtaposed or superimposed. The chromium-plated hinge-handle allows the leaf (in glass or wood) to slide into the upper groove. The modules shown at the 1929 Salon des Artistes Décorateurs were as revolutionary as those exhibited by Le Corbusier, but the careful choice of material – black-lacquered limewood – is a distinctively Ruhlmann touch.

Collectionneur stool. 1925. Part of the furniture for the music room. Aubusson tapestry by Gaudissard.

Morel dressing-table. 1921–22. Ref. 1522 AR/1825 NR. Named after an architect in Ruhlmann's earliest team. Two cavity drawers with sliding lids frame the tabletop, which is decorated with a circle of ivory pearls. The dressing-table illustrated is in macassar ebony; others were made in mahogany, rosewood and bur ash.

Eléphant chair. 1926 and 1931. In black. A successful model which Ruhlmann used again in the office of Maréchal Lyautey.

Fuseau secretaire. Circa 1925. Ref. 1544 AR/1607 NR. Macassar ebony, interior lined with doeskin, folding leaf inlaid with tortoiseshell. The ribbed *fuseau* legs extend almost to the top of the curved frame, which narrows as it nears the pediment.

Large fluted commode. Macassar ebony. The frame was sculpted and then laminated so as to catch the light, and the whole piece seems to be suspended between the *fuseau* legs. Photograph taken in 1923 at the salon des Artistes Décorateurs in the Pavillon de Marsan, where the commode was shown for the first time.

Cigar boxes. Ref. 4239 and 4238 NR. These silver-bronze boxes might have been made by a great goldsmith. The ogee moulded lid belongs to model 4238 NR, which has a handle decorated with a pebbled relief. Model 4238 is in the collection of Michael Chow.

LA DÉCORATION
CHEZ
RUHLMANN

27, rue de Lisbonne, 27

RUHLMANN
AS
DECORATOR

From furniture to interior design. One comment in Vaudoyer's account of the 1919 Salon d'Automne stands out and clearly indicates that something new was happening: 'The neologisms of the interior decorators have a lot to do with the favourable reception given to modern furniture.'

Although their innovations may have aroused doubts in some minds, they would have delighted Raymond Koechlin. The superiority of the Germans at the Turin exhibition was based upon the close links between all the decorative arts and upon the participants' willingness to provide complete modern interiors that were ready to be lived in.[1] Koechlin noted that the French had fallen victim to a cult of the past, that they were paralysed by their individualism. They were capable of creating individual pieces of furniture, but had difficulty in designing complete interiors: 'There is no such thing as a modern salon. The public will turn to modernism only when modernism gives it the one room in which its ceremonies take place.'

But if the furniture designer was to change public attitudes and create a new environment, he had to do more than simply become an 'interior designer'. In accordance with the principles established by those who had created the various monarchical styles – Le Brun under Louis XIV, Percier with the Empire style – Ruhlmann wanted to harmonize every element in his interiors: furniture, wallpaper, lighting, carpets.

Did this ambition imply aesthetic tyranny? In any event, a controversy soon broke out between those who thought the designer should be in complete control and those who rejected such interference because it would frustrate personal initiative.[2] With fifty years' hindsight, it seems obvious that the interior decorators would never have created and established the Art Déco style if they had not, like Ruhlmann, had the ambition to combine the functions of 'master of works', designer and decorator. The rooms they decorated were a further incitement to introduce new ideas without necessarily doing away with antique furniture and paintings. Both the SAD (Société des Artistes Décorateurs) and the UCAD (Union Centrale des Arts Décoratifs) encouraged any move away from individualism and informality.

In a praiseworthy attempt at cooperation, Ruhlmann, Sue et Mare and Follot furnished a large reception room at the 1921 Salon d'Automne. The

1 Shortly before the opening of the exhibition, it was noticed that France was exhibiting only reproduction antique furniture. At the last moment, Charles Plumet improvised a 'Pavillon des arts décoratifs contemporains' and asked artists to lend their creations. The opening was delayed by a month.
2 'Designing a whole interior as though it were a set is a form of tyranny. Not one of the carefully placed elements can be moved without destroying the desired stylistic effect', G. Janneau, *La Renaissance de l'art français*, January 1921.

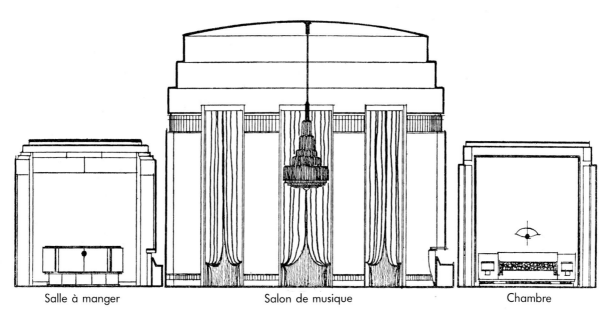

Salle à manger   Salon de musique   Chambre

Section of the Hôtel du Collectionneur, 1925, showing how
Patout and Ruhlmann used a stepped construction to conform to
the height regulations and to vary the height of the ceiling from
room to room.

Design for a hall, 1924.

theme set for the 1924 UCAD exhibition was 'a lady's boudoir', and each designer tried to create an atmosphere of refined intimacy, harmonizing furniture, hangings, objets d'art, carpets and lights. For its part, the committee responsible for French exhibitions held abroad decided to appoint an architect and a designer who would be jointly responsible for design coordination. Ruhlmann acted as coordinator on several occasions (notably in Barcelona in 1923 and 1928).

The fact remains, however, that the major priorities of all the leading decorators were finding a personal style and keeping their customers. All the interiors of the period have an Art Déco atmosphere, but it is impossible to speak of any unity of style. As the catalogue for the fiftieth anniversary of the Exposition des Arts Décoratifs points out, '1925 offers us an incredible diversity of styles and creations, a whole storehouse of ideas from which we can still learn. . . It is no accident that now that we live in a universe designed by Le Corbusier and his friends we look back with nostalgia to Sue et Mare, Ruhlmann, Rateau and Jacques Doucet's team.'

From decoration to interior architecture. Layman though he was, Ruhlmann was obviously passionately interested in architecture. Thanks to his friends Tauzin, Boileau, Marozeau and above all his life-long friend Pierre Patout, the young decorator acquired an elementary knowledge of architecture which allowed him to imagine how his furniture would look when in place, to plan complete rooms and to sketch interiors and buildings.

Tenders for construction work and commissions for decorating and furnishing houses brought Ruhlmann into constant contact with architects, and he absorbed their ability to mould space, play on contrasts and vary proportions so as to give each room an appropriate volume. In short, he was able to see things from an architectural rather than a purely decorative point of view. Significantly enough, when he decided to become a furniture-designer, he recruited a team of draughtsmen and architects rather than one of cabinet-makers. Few of his architects had completed their studies; Ruhlmann preferred new talent to official qualifications.[3]

Ruhlmann insisted that the names of the twelve collaborators who had helped establish his reputation as a designer should appear in *Documents d'architecture*, which describes the interiors he created between

3 J.H. Le Même was a student at the Atelier Pascal and at the age of twenty-six won a competition open to all students at the Ecole des Beaux-Arts. His design for a private swimming pool delighted Ruhlmann, who took him on immediately. Le Même was to stay with Ruhlmann for three years. In 1926 he qualified and won the Prix Blumenthal and then left Ruhlmann to work in Mégève.

1913 and 1924. Five of the twelve were architects (Baudrier, Le Même, Morel, Haranger, Porteneuve) and the others were draughtsmen (Stephany, Huet, Bougenot, Pico, Lardin, Lautelin and Denise Nolin).

Whereas the architects stayed at the rue de Lisbonne only until such time as they had completed their theoretical training, the draughtsmen often spent their entire careers with Ruhlmann and became permanently marked by his style. On his death in 1934, most of them set up on their own, but they rarely succeeded in shaking off his influence. The term 'Ruhlmannisme' was still in use in the early fifties, and it cannot be denied that Ruhlmann established a real following.[4]

Even when he was working with architects, Ruhlmann still retained the conceptual initiative. It was he who issued the directives to realize projects drawn up in discussions with clients and finalized on site. Plans, perspective drawings and elevations were then drawn up. These included access plans and notes on furniture and decorative themes. The gouache, pen and ink and charcoal maquettes were then bound with raw silk cords into albums which provide an invaluable record of the style of the houses created by a man who gradually became a true master of interior architecture.[5]

Even when he asked Pierre Patout to take responsibility for a building, Ruhlmann remained in charge of the overall project. Thus, the first study for the 1925 Hôtel du Collectionneur appears in a sketchbook dating from 1919: a perfectly classical pavilion which is reminiscent of Bagatelle or Butard. A publication dealing with the building describes Patout as the architect and Ruhlmann as 'master of works'.

4 'Several decorators who currently enjoy a certain prestige have been influenced by Ruhlmann, but they cannot equal him. They are trying to perpetuate an art which, as transposed by them, is rich but not precious, conscientious but not stylish. The problem is that it is not given to everyone to possess the constantly innovatory imagination, the sense of grandeur and finesse, the sense of harmony and the dignity that made Ruhlmann an artist in the true sense of the word.' 'Ruhlmannisme', *Art présent*, 1947.
5 Once the project had been costed and adopted, the work of the craftsmen was supervised by the drawing office. Every decision had to be countersigned by Ruhlmann, who saw to it personally that the commission went well. His presence was constantly felt in the drawing office.

Hôtel du Collectionneur, 1925. The same classical inspiration can be seen in this sketch dating from 1919 and in Patout's preliminary design. According to Léon Deshairs, 'The architect could not build the complete house he wanted to build or a house that could be lived in. He had to use temporary materials such as plaster and staff rather than stone and concrete. He never saw his white façades surrounded by the greenery of a garden. But it has to be admitted that he arrived at a happy compromise between a real house and an exhibition pavilion.'

The Hôtel du Collectionneur. The Hôtel du Collectionneur, which was admired by millions of visitors to the Exposition Internationale des Arts Décoratifs in 1925, confirmed Ruhlmann's supremacy and gave him an international audience. Even today, it is still seen as the most representative product of Art Déco.

In his attempts to harmonize architecture, decoration, furniture and objets d'art, Ruhlmann had to coordinate the work of some forty artists and forty tradesmen. Not a single detail escaped the attention of this indefatigable 'master of works'.[6]

The initial plan drawn up in collaboration with Pierre Patout was for a two-storey house surrounded by gardens. It was, unfortunately, to be demolished after the exhibition and was therefore built in temporary materials. It finally took the form of a single-storey building adapted to allow the crowds to walk around inside it. The bedrooms planned for the first floor, and the basement service areas, were never built.

In order to respect the height requirements imposed to preserve a clear view of the Invalides,[7] Patout opted for a stepped construction with an overall height of ten metres. He was thus able to compress the elevation and ground plan into an octagon inscribed within an eighteen-metre square. The external appearance of the building was determined by the requirements of scale and by the distribution and form of the rooms. The salon was eight metres high, with the bedroom and dining room scaled to one half, and the bathroom to one third, of its height. The proportions guaranteed that the atmosphere would be personal and that the restricted space would appear roomy. The same desire to break up the monotony governed the equilibrium of the façades and the sober use of ornamentation. Solids dominate the voids: the rotunda is relieved by three tall bay windows and a frieze by Joseph Bertrand, and flanked by two low porticoes which housed frescoes by Henri Marret. The sculptured group of women by Janniot in front of the building seemed to place the Hôtel du Collectionneur under the symbolic patronage of the Renaissance sculptor Jean Goujon, probably the artist who was most successful in reconciling modernity with French tradition. Skilfully playing upon cultural references and measured contrasts, Ruhlmann

6 The names of the artists associated with the Hôtel du Collectionneur appear in the circular gallery and in publications dealing with it. They included the sculptors Bourdelle, J. Bernard, Dejean, Despiau, Pompon and Poisson; the painters Dupas, Rigal and Marret; Brandt, craftsman in wrought iron; the furniture designers Jallot, Rapin and Sognot. The carpets and tapestries were by Gaudissard, Reboussin and Voguet; the fabrics by Stephany, lacquer work by Dunand; ceramics by Decoeur, Mayodon and Lenoble; silverware by Bastard and Puiforcat; glassware by Marinot.
7 The façades of buildings constructed on the Esplanade des Invalides could be no higher than 5.2m and the pitch of their roofs was restricted to 45°. This explains why so many of the pavilions were surmounted by domes or cupolas to allow use of the greatest possible volume.

Patout's preliminary design for the Hôtel du Collectionneur, 1925.

Janniot's *Hommage à Jean Goujon* stands in front of the rotunda. The three bas reliefs by Foucault on the curved panel above the windows illustrate the theme of *La Danse*. The four tiers that frame the great oval salon define the distribution of the rooms and allow the ceiling height to be varied: this breaks the monotony and gives each room an atmosphere of its own.

succeeded in catalysing all the major tendencies within Art Déco. As one critic put it, alluding to Victor Hugo's devastating 1827 manifesto of the New Age in literature, the Hôtel du Collectionneur was 'the ''Préface de *Cromwell*'' of the new art of decoration'.

Hôtel du Collectionneur, 1925. Boudoir, between the bedroom and the bathroom. Its green, white and gold harmonies are enhanced by the small pieces of dark furniture. The *réchampi* panelling, the corner mirrors with their contemporary ornaments, and the white marble fireplace with its green and gold overmantle all recall the *petits appartements* of the eighteenth century. The ceiling is a low oval cupola surrounded by a gilded dentil. The delicate tripod table, the light-coloured silk coverings of the wing chair and *causeuse*, and the precious roll-top desk (not shown) all combine to create the intimate atmosphere one expects of a boudoir. Part of the bathroom can be seen in the background.

Hôtel du Collectionneur, 1925. Bedroom. The room is hung with ivory damask, and the blue-greys of the ceiling and the woodwork harmonize with the pink and blue carpet designed by Voguet. The wing chair, the bed and the bur amboina-wood bedside tables are all covered in fur. The large ebony macassar and ivory commode stands opposite a *fuseau* dressing-table (not visible in the photograph). The distinguished modernism of this room remains undated.

Hôtel du Collectionneur, 1925. Salon. The great oval salon is entered through wrought-iron doors by Brandt. It is the nerve centre of the building and is dedicated to music. The cupola, with paintings illustrating Beethoven's symphonies, is bordered by a fluted grey and gold band. A macassar ebony grand piano by Gaveau stands beneath it. The pedals are supported by a silver bronze lyre. The window frames are gilded. The walls are hung with a silk lampas by Stephany, its carmine motifs harmonizing with the plain rose and blue of Gaudissard's immense carpet. A painting by Dupas hangs over the 'peachblossom' marble fireplace. The room is lit by six wall lamps in silver bronze with clusters of crystal pearls. Like the chandelier, they were designed by Ruhlmann and executed by Viau. Various chairs by Rapin, Sognot and Jallot complete the furnishings.

Hôtel du Collectionneur, 1925. Salon. To the right, one of the three bay windows making up the rotunda can be seen. The drapes are in light grey silk. Bourdelle's *Herakles* stands on a large lacquered cabinet by Dunand after Lambert-Rucki. The chairs are covered in Aubusson tapestry after a cartoon by Gaudissard and have the solemn dignity of Empire furniture.

This is obviously not a design, but a sketch made
by Ruhlmann during his travels.

Design for a hall. Sketchbook
3, dated 1913. Reproduced,
Moussinac, pl. 53.

Evolution of style 1913–1920: Studio style; boudoir style. The fact that Ruhlmann became interested in decoration very early in his career tells us nothing about how he arranged his room as a young man or how he furnished the apartment he took when he was first married. Nor do we know anything of the wallpaper he exhibited on Selmersheim's stand in 1910, but the name of that architect, together with that of Plumet, may give us some clues. Both encouraged Ruhlmann to realize his ambitions, and both were apostles of 'social' art. Ruhlmann's early style is completely different from the luxurious refinements which characterize the work of the mature designer. The design for a 'hall in Normandy' (dated 1914), with its exposed beams, sculpted wooden staircase and simple but comfortable furniture, has a somewhat English rustic charm. As it was designed for the artist's small country house in Normandy, it must have appealed to his personal taste.

The dining room shown at the 1913 Salon d'Automne is less rustic, but its simplicity is equally surprising. Whereas the other exhibitors, with the exception of Poiret, tried to find a modern equivalent to nineteenth-century styles, Ruhlmann disconcerted the critics, who saw him as a disciple of the Munich school. The boudoir and studio rooms he favoured at this time were inspired by an absence of formality. The intimate atmosphere is suggested by the wide divans, the brocaded cushions and the light colours. The 'study' elements – table, bookshelf and armchair – are concentrated in the working area. Space is rounded into recesses, groined vaults and alcoves; horizontals are more important than verticals, comfort takes precedence over decorum. The same characteristics can be seen in the boudoir-library of 1918, even though the 'couturier' style is softened by the designer's desire to highlight the cabinet-work. The transition is less obvious in the boudoir-alcove and in a sketch for a stage set (both 1918), in which the influence of the Ballets Russes is still evident. The hangings, drapes, cushions, carpets and the intense shimmering colours create an extremely attractive 'artistic' disorder which Ruhlmann was soon to abandon.

The quality and sobriety of his furniture made a considerable impression at the 1919 Salon d'Automne. The days of the 'tapissier' style were over. The architect was beginning to take over from the dilettante whose one desire was to please. A rigorous stylist was beginning to emerge.

Set design showing the influence of the Ballets Russes.

Design for a boudoir. Indian ink, gouache, with gold highlights.
Circa 1920.

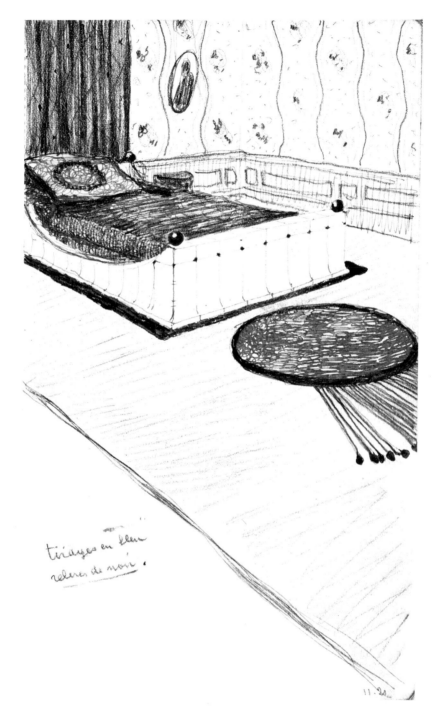

Bedroom. Sketch dated 1913. Sketchbook 5.

Apartment of the dress-designer Fernande Cabanel. The decorator's style is still marked by a combination of shimmering hangings (influenced by the Ballets Russes) and the furs and heaped cushions associated with Paul Poiret. The photograph shows some of Ruhlmann's most representative 'precious' furniture: the Lafleur bed, Cabanel chiffonier, Araignée and Basse-Boule tables and a Stèle desk. The chandelier is covered in printed silk by Fortuny.

Gouache, 1923. Ref. Intérieur 4E 32. Published in *Harmonies*, pl. 23.

Boudoir-library, 1918. *Harmonies de Ruhlmann*, pl. 12.

1922–1928: Luxury apartments. Ruhlmann the decorator worked out the basic elements of the luxury apartment in the early twenties, before the Hôtel du Collectionneur became the symbol of the Ruhlmann house. The change was almost total: the refinements became extremely subtle, and 'artistic' disorder gave way to an orderly sobriety.[8]

Implicitly governed by the *ancien régime* principle of making a distinction between *petits appartements* and *grands appartements*, private apartments and state apartments, the distribution of the rooms and service areas means that reception areas and living areas can be kept separate. The diversity of premises (private houses and flats which all pose different problems), the need to convert an existing interior rather than constructing it, and the need to adapt to the personality and life-style of the owners all mean that the interior designer has to have a certain psychological sensitivity. It was that sensitivity which enabled Ruhlmann to reconcile the aesthetic desires of his clients with his own projects.

The initial problem posed by the luxury apartment is that of space. There are a large number of rooms, and some of them have subsidiary rooms attached: the bedroom has its boudoir, the study its antechamber and the bathroom its lounging area. The spaces are very large, but the height of the ceiling can be adapted to the volume of the room with infinite subtlety. Each of the rooms designed by Ruhlmann is entered via a passageway. Bedrooms and boudoirs are entered through low, enclosed passageways which create a calculated contrast between the two areas. The entrances through to large, richly furnished areas take the form of peristyles. Side elevations of Ruhlmann houses show how regularly he alternated between the two.

Even the style of the working drawings changes. The frontal perspective disappears and is replaced by an angular perspective, as though the room were seen through a wide-angle lens. The horizon is lowered almost to floor level. As a result the verticals and horizontals are emphasized and the feeling of distance is distorted.

Ruhlmann's interest in adapting rooms to specific purposes led him to create specifically masculine and feminine harmonies, which emphasize sociability and intimacy respectively. In both cases, there is a certain theatricality: day-beds are placed in front of lacquered screens; fireplaces, secretaires and *causeuses* are grouped together in a confined space.

8 As artistic adviser to Primavera, Ruhlmann created a 'swimming pool for a villa on the Côte d'Azur' in collaboration with a team from Printemps. It was the main attraction at the 1924 Salon d'Automne. The extraordinary luxury of this stand may have had more to do with Ruhlmann than with Louis Sognot or Alfred Levard, the store's decorator and architect respectively.

The solemn atmosphere is heightened by the use of wall panelling, usually in rosewood, and by the monumental effect created by the introduction of fluting, coffered vaulting and pillars which stand against the walls. The Hôtel du Collectionneur is a celebration of Ruhlmann's sumptuous taste, as are the two rooms seen at the Salon des Artistes Décorateurs (SAD): an office exhibited in 1926 and a luxury bedroom shown in 1928.

Preliminary study for the office of Maréchal Lyautey. 1929.

Boudoir. *Harmonies de Ruhlmann*, pl. 21.

Hall. *Harmonies de Ruhlmann*, pl.3.

The return to simplicity. It is quite possible that Ruhlmann's 1928 'state' bedroom indirectly contributed to the break-up of the SAD. Ruhlmann wanted the room to be almost outrageously luxurious, and for several years the antagonism between neo-classicists and modernists had suggested that a break was unavoidable, given the crystallization of both tendencies.

In 1929, the very year in which the dissidents founded the Union des Artistes Modernes (UAM),[9] Ruhlmann began to change his style, although there is no reason to suspect him of opportunism. He turned away from luxury and hyperbolic refinements, adapting his talents to social change and to the implications of the growing economic crisis.

The change was probably not apparent to the visitors who flocked to see Ruhlmann's stand at the 1929 Salon des Artistes Décorateurs. The subject itself invited hyperbole: it was, after all, a design for a 'study in the Cité Universitaire for a crown prince, the Viceroy of India'.

Ruhlmann concentrated on progress and comfort.[10] Although the furniture is scaled for the hall in which it is set and is therefore of considerable dimensions, the individual pieces seem small and appear to be surrounded by empty space. In his own way, Ruhlmann was following Francis Jourdain's advice to 'unfurnish'.[11] Each element becomes a centre for a specific activity: a desk for work, modular boxes for storage, a chaise-longue for relaxation and a games table for leisure.

Ruhlmann was no longer afraid to challenge the traditions of *ébénisterie*. He also began to furnish his own imposingly simple office at this time. The two windows face two double doors in dark lacquer which are relieved only by the chromium plating of the shields which serve as doorknobs. The black lacquer furniture is not unrelated to that designed for the 'Viceroy of India' (the desk and modular bookcase are in fact the same). One unexpected innovation was introduced: the radiators are not concealed. They stand in the centre of the room and function as pedestals supporting two tall vases in Sèvres porcelain which provide concealed lighting. The soft warm colours of the large sunburst carpet provide a counterpoint to the contrasting black and white.

9 The UAM had six founder members: Hélène Henry, Pierre Chareau, René Herbst, Francis Jourdain, Robert Mallet-Stevens and Raymond Templier. Its first exhibition was held a year later in the Pavillon de Marsan.
10 'Although the majestic appearance of the studio which adjoins the more intimate bedroom relates to the artist's usual themes and his aristocratic tastes, everything in it is subordinated to practical needs in accordance with modern taste and modern customs.' René Chavance, *Art et décoration*, July 1929.
11 'It is as possible to fit out a room luxuriously by unfurnishing it as by furnishing it. The great decorators of the future will restrict themselves to purely necessary elements, but those elements will be perfectly proportioned and balanced and the room will not seem bare.' Francis Jourdain, cited by René Chavance, *Art et décoration*, January 1922.

Ruhlmann's last great creation, at the 1932 Salon des Artistes Décorateurs, symbolizes his return to an almost rustic simplicity. We know that his 'Rendez-vous de pêcheurs de truites' was a design for his country house in Normandy. This huge construction included a dining room, a lounge area with a fireplace and, on the mezzanine floor, a room with twin beds. Contemporary observers were at once disconcerted by and drawn to the solid cherry-wood furniture, the straw-bottomed chairs and the print curtains that evoked the comforts of a country house. Ruhlmann seemed to have come a long way from the style of decoration he himself had set. By a roundabout route he had come back to the sturdy independence which had always allowed him to express his true personality.

The 'Rendez-vous de Pecheurs de Truites' (Trout-fishers' rendezvous) was without doubt the most impressive stand at the 1932 Salon des Artistes Décorateurs. Despite the economic crisis, Ruhlmann spent 40,000 francs on it. He decorated and furnished 'a large hall with a dining table, a dresser, fireside chairs, a games table, a large fireplace with andirons, tongs and gridiron, racks for fishing rods, a gun rack and a radio. The bedroom on the first floor has a dressing-table which doubles as a writing desk, a commode and beds' (from the invitation composed by Ruhlmann for the opening of the Salon des Artistes Décorateurs).

'Rendez-vous de Pêcheurs de Truites.' Table, 1932. Ref. 1317 NR. This round table in solid cherry-wood with a pedestal in the form of a wine-press marks Ruhlmann's return to an almost rustic simplicity.

'Rendez-vous de Pêcheurs de Truites.' Hall.

Ruhlmann's contributions to national and international exhibitions

1911 Exhibits wallpaper on Tony Selmersheim's stand at the Salon des Artistes Décorateurs (SAD).

1913 Salon d'Automne: dining room; various 'classic' pieces shown in a circular gallery (Doucet *bergère*, Triplan secretaire).

1919 SAD, Pavillon de Marsan: Stèle dressing-table; Salon d'Automne: *Meuble au Char*, various pieces and maquettes. Exhibits in Strasbourg.

1920 SAD, Pavillon de Marsan: *vide-poche* in amaranth, ivory and ebony. Salon d'Automne: sideboard with amboina-wood veneer and ivory marquetry (Elysée).

1921 SAD, Pavillon de Marsan: *Table-vasque* (basin/table) in sculpted macassar, macassar ebony, top in amaranth with ivory marquetry. Salon d'Automne: various precious pieces, including the fluted commode and the small *fuseau* jewellery cabinet.

1922 SAD, Pavillon de Marsan: macassar sideboard table *Meuble au Char*, three-leaf cheval-glass in bur amboina-wood, half-moon commode in sycamore with ivory marquetry. Salon d'Automne: precious furniture in macassar ebony. Exhibits in Amsterdam.

1923 SAD, Grand Palais: roll-top desk in macassar ebony with ivory marquetry, interior in coral. Exposition d'Art Décoratif Contemporain, Pavillon de Marsan: Hydravion (Seaplane) armchair and 'an imposing sideboard in macassar ebony'. Salon d'Automne: two-tier kidney-shaped desk (David-Weill) in amboina-wood, ivory and shagreen (sold for 9,900 francs). International exhibitions: Monza, Barcelona and Rio de Janeiro.

1924 SAD: Colette commode, Fontane chiffonier, Ref. 1533 AR/2232 NR (now in the Musée des Arts Décoratifs); various pieces in a hall/dining room designed in collaboration with Chareau (theme: 'reception and intimacy in a modern apartment'). UCDA: Pavillon de Marsan: Lady's boudoir, Tibattant secretaire and wingchair (Collectionneur boudoir). Salon d'Automne: divan in Comblanchien limetone, in collaboration with Primavera.

1925 Exposition Internationale des Arts Décoratifs et Industriels Modernes: Hôtel du Collectionneur. SAD: office library for an embassy in collaboration with Boileau and Carrière (architects).

1926 'Collector's study' with semi-metallic desk and bookcase, Rasson piece, secretaires in ebony and tortoiseshell and amboina-wood and tortoiseshell, Eléphant armchairs and *canapés*. Salon d'Automne: Duval collector's chest, ebony macassar with tortoiseshell doors, interior lined with grey doeskin. Ref. 1511 AR/2300 NR.

Dining room at the 1913 Salon d'Automne.

1927 Exhibits in Madrid and Milan.

1928 SAD: 'State' bedroom with *lit-corbeille*. Exhibits in Athens and Barcelona.

1929 SAD: 'Study bedroom for a crown prince, the Viceroy of India, in the Cité Universitaire', including the black lacquer furniture – Tardieu desk and bed, modular bookcase – later made in macassar ebony for the Maharajah of Indore; supervises the 'feminine arts' room.

1930 SAD: dressing-room for Jacqueline Francel: dressing-table in glass, chrome and violet-wood, chiffonier and secretaire in violet-wood. Exhibition of furniture and sculpture in the rue de Lisbonne.

Salon d'Automne, 1924. Exhibit designed in collaboration with Primavera. Peristyle of swimming-pool.

1931 Exposition Coloniale: Office for Maréchal Lyautey. Exhibition in the rue de Lisbonne.

1932 SAD: 'Rendez-vous de pêcheurs de truites' – salon, dining room and bedroom. The stand cost 400,000 francs. Salon d'Automne: maquettes for sets and props for Géraldy's play *Christine*, which opened at the Comédie Française.

1933 SAD: lady's desk, violet-wood and morocco, matching chair.

1934 Retrospective held in the Pavillon de Marsan.

Salon d'Automne, 1924. This classical day-bed, designed by Ruhlmann in 1917 and seen in a design for a bathroom dated 1918, is here theatrically placed in front of mosaic columns framing a sculpture by Joseph Bernard. A hand-woven carpet leads from the swimming pool to the bed.

Salon d'Automne, 1924. The most spectacular and the most widely praised stand was that designed by Primavera in collaboration with Ruhlmann. The architect Levard and the designer-decorator designed a swimming pool for a villa on the Côte d'Azur with columns, ornamental vases and a marble staircase leading from the pool to the salon-boudoir.

Salon des Artistes Décorateurs, 1926. This view of the work area of the 'collector's study' gives some idea of the size of Ruhlmann's stand (peristyle, furniture, *canapé*. . .). The photograph shows Eléphant armchairs, the Nicolle cabinet and, in front of the monumental fresco by Dupas, a semi-metallic bookcase and desk in solid macassar ebony with a silver-chrome frame.

Salon des Artistes Décorateurs, 1928. The oval-shaped 'state' bedroom is lit by a sumptuous crystal chandelier and by strip lighting concealed in the cornice. A day-bed and a tripod table can be seen in the foreground.

Salon des Artistes Décorateurs, 1928. 'State' bedroom. The dressing-table is in shagreen, violet-wood and macassar ebony. The mirror folds down to form a writing platform. Curtains in raw silk.

Salon des Artistes Décorateurs, 1928. The 'state' bedroom is furnished with a dressing-table and with two oval sets of drawers on scroll bases on either side of the amboina-wood cheval-glass. The Hussarde commode and the crystal chandelier are reflected in the mirror. The walls are hung with the silk lampas from the music room in the Hôtel du Collectionneur.

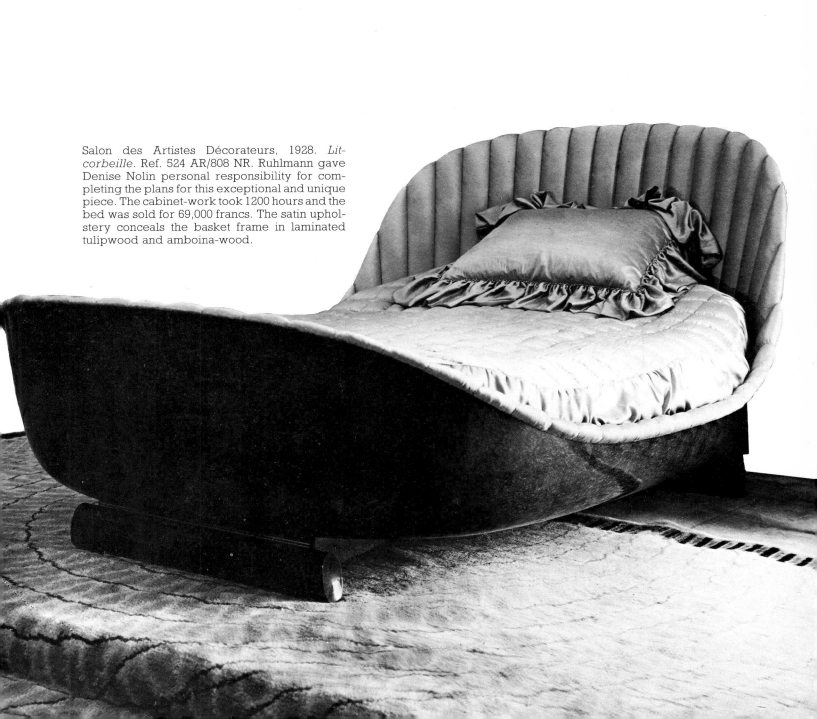

Salon des Artistes Décorateurs, 1928. *Lit-corbeille*. Ref. 524 AR/808 NR. Ruhlmann gave Denise Nolin personal responsibility for completing the plans for this exceptional and unique piece. The cabinet-work took 1200 hours and the bed was sold for 69,000 francs. The satin upholstery conceals the basket frame in laminated tulipwood and amboina-wood.

Salon des Artistes Décorateurs, 1929. 'Study bedroom for a crown prince, the Viceroy of India, in the Cité Universitaire', combining areas for work, leisure and rest. The simple, low furniture is in wood covered with black industrial lacquer.

Salon des Artistes Décorateurs, 1930. Dressing-room designed for Jacqueline Francel. The rounded shape of the room and the large 'sunburst' carpet lead the eye to the astonishing make-up table in which Ruhlmann combines traditional *ébénisterie* (violet-wood) with non-conventional materials (glass and chrome). The metal chair, which bears no resemblance to the traditional dressing-table chair, also combines modernity and functionalism.

Exposition Coloniale, 1931. Constructed by the architects Laprade and Jaussely for the 1931 exhibition, the permanent Musée des Colonies comprises two salons linked by a gallery. One salon was furnished by Printz, the other by Ruhlmann. The latter later became Maréchal Lyautey's office. Bouquet's fresco illustrates Africa's contribution to world culture.

Exposition Coloniale, 1931. Maréchal Lyautey's desk in the bay window. The desk is a Bloch in macassar ebony and shagreen made by Jules Deroubaix in 1928-1929.

The Chambre de Commerce, Paris. In 1926, Ruhlmann won an open competition to decorate two adjoining wings in the Hôtel Potocki, which houses the Chambre de Commerce. He had to take into account both the Second Empire architecture and the conservative tastes of the committee.

The rounded debating and conference chamber is lit by a glass roof and by strip lights concealed behind the cornice and the panelling. The walls are covered with hangings designed by Stephany (rose on a silver ground), and a modern Gobelins tapestry covers the panel behind the president's chair. The decorations are completed by a few wall lamps in silvered bronze and alabaster.

In the centre is a large table in natural oak (a variant on the Ambassade 1925 desk) and the conference seating on a slightly raised dais forms an ellipse. The whole has the gravity and sobriety one would expect of a room in which important representatives of the business world meet.

The ballroom (Salle des Fêtes), completed shortly afterwards in 1927, created problems because of its dimensions. It is extremely wide – thirteen metres – and its height (eight metres) is inadequate. Its proportions are the exact opposite of those of the Galerie des Glaces at Versailles. In order to remove the impression of heaviness, Ruhlmann narrowed the room by placing a double row of fluted columns between the windows. The low entablatures form a concave curve above the cornice and make the ceiling look higher than it actually is. The room is lit by strip lights concealed behind the cornice and by two rows of six chandeliers similar to those in the Hôtel du Collectionneur.

G. Varenne, *Art et décoration*, January–June 1928.

The door facing the stage which closes off one end of the ballroom is surmounted by a bas-relief by Joseph Bertrand (*La Danse*). In order to ensure that this large room was both warm and cheerful, Ruhlmann did not use marble, but 'gold-green panelling relieved by moulded staff medallions designed in collaboration with Hairon. The mouldings, the cornice and the main decorative motifs are picked out in gold. The pink ceiling is heavily grained. The long curtains are pure green.'

Faced with a delicate architectural problem and with the need to respect official canons of beauty, Ruhlmann combined decorous solemnity and the charm of a room used for balls and elegant festivities.

Chambre de Commerce, 1927. Conference chamber. The central table is a variation on the 1925 Ambassade desk.

New York City Bank, Paris, *c.* 1930. Work area.

Chambre de Commerce, 1927. Conference chamber.

New York City Bank, Paris, *c*. 1930. An austere and geometrical room, in which the verticals predominate. The impression of space is created by the compact furniture and is heightened by the tall window.

Chambre de Commerce, 1927. Fitted out by
Ruhlmann, this ballroom was inspired by the
Galerie des Glaces at Versailles and combines
architectural and decorative elements.

Ile de France. Companionway on B Deck. The decorator created an impression of space, accentuating the verticals by introducing columns veneered in light ash-wood and stressing the contrast between the geometrically coffered ceiling and the sinuous curve of the floor.

The liner Ile de France. In 1927, the Compagnie Générale Transatlantique (founded in 1864) launched France's largest liner, the *Ile de France*. On 22 June, the new giant of the seas left Le Havre with two thousand guests on board. The ship was a floating city and an ambassador for the decorative arts of France. The best decorators in France were commissioned, each being given personal responsiblity for decorating a public room or a particular type of cabin. The reading and writing room was decorated by Leleu and the lounge by Sue et Mare. Ruhlmann coordinated the corridors linking the first class salons, the main stairway and the great hall. The latter had adjoining rest areas and games areas. It was normally used as a *salon de thé*, and occasionally for receptions like that held to celebrate the liner's maiden voyage.

Ile de France. First-class *salon de thé* in the reception hall. The white staff ceiling is divided into shallow coffers to reflect the light from the tall vases on their cuboid pedestals. Ruhlmann restores the vertical balance of this vast room by accentuating the chromatic contrast between the ceiling, which is bathed in light, and the green and pink tints of the marbled ash panelling. The pilasters, which are also in ash, have silver bronze capitals and emphasize the architectural note. The engraved, frosted and sand-blasted blind windows help to conceal the fact that the hall is in fact below the waterline.

Ile de France. Passageway leading to the *salon de thé*. The walls are panelled in varnished white ash, and the rectangular mirrors make the passageway look wider than it really is. The walls are hung with antique maps and engravings.

Ile de France. Head of the main stairway linking B, C and D decks. The wrought-iron banister is by Raymond Subes. The coffered ceilings and ash panelling provide continuity with the *salon de thé*. Jean Dupas's painting based upon Nerval's *Sylvie*, which is set in the Ile de France, is reflected in the large mirror.

Ile de France. Janniot's sculpture, which stands in front of the stairway, also evokes the Ile de France. The woman is supported by a stag. This gigantic couple in stone symbolizes bucolic happiness. Like the chairs and couches, the pedestal tables and games tables were specially designed to adapt to the rolling of the liner.

Ile de France. One of the two games rooms off the reception hall. The narrow panels in dark red industrial lacquer simulate the ribs of an umbrella and give a false impression of height. Indirect lighting is provided by the alabaster vases on top of the lamp standards.

Windburn. Circa 1928. Salon-Library.

Haardt. 1927-28. Design for a salon communicating with the study.

Lord Rothermere. Circa 1925. Hall-salon, Paris. Two groups of four rosewood-panelled columns form a peristyle between the two rooms.

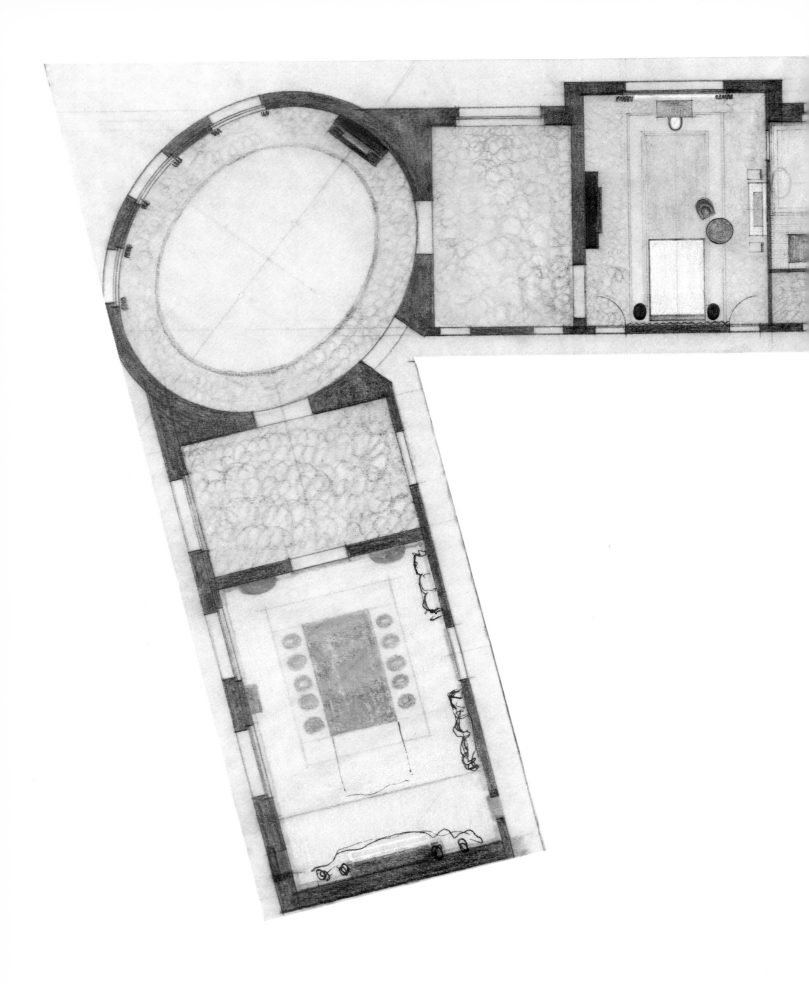

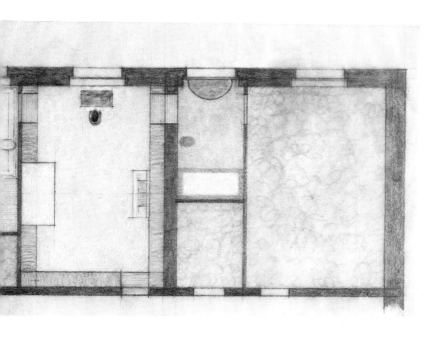

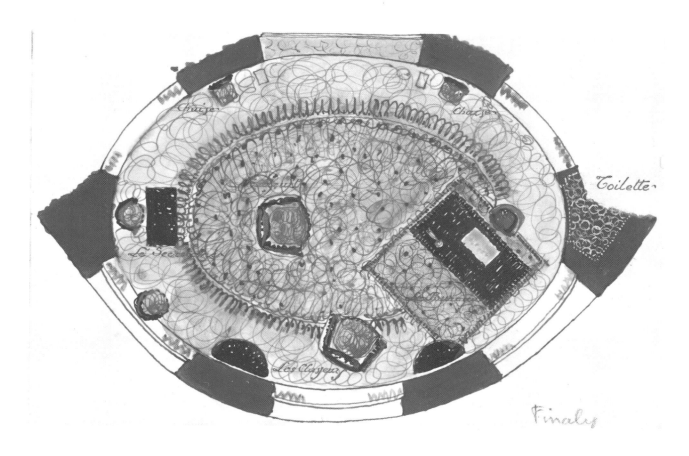

Finaly design. The rooms in this apartment are
arranged around the salon in the oval rotunda.

Hôtel Ducharne, rue Albéric-Magnard, La Muette (Paris). The house, built by Patout just before the Exposition des Arts Décoratifs, is reminiscent of the Hôtel du Collectionneur. The banister describes a perfect arabesque and plays upon the contrasting materials and colours (marble and metal). The walls of the salon and the *bergères* are covered in silk specially designed for François Ducharne, a famous silk manufacturer from Lyon, producing primarily for the haute couture industry, 'who weaves the sun, the moon and the blue rays of the rain' (Colette).

Hôtel Ducharne. The main hall is designed as an art gallery. In later years François Ducharne acquired a fine collection of modern paintings and sculptures, including the Rodin bronze seen in the foreground.

Hôtel Ducharne. Dining room. This room recalls the design and furnishings of the Hôtel du Collectionneur. Table with double lyre support; silver cabinet with the lock plate created by Foucault for the Elysée sideboard.

Fricotelle. 1926-27. Dining room. The dark panelling of the walls provides a contrast with the recessed square panels of the ceiling. The furniture is in bur amboina-wood: oval table with a double scroll base, chairs and a Collectionneur silver-cabinet.

Fricotelle. Hall and Salon; showing changes in style between the early twenties and the early thirties. The Salon was completed by Porteneuve. The furniture is by Ruhlmann.

Berger. Paris, 1923. Ruhlmann designed this rosewood panelling for one of his main suppliers of precious woods. At the insistence of the client, a coffered vault was added, not without difficulty. The dominant tone is relieved only by the carpet and the amboina-wood table, which has a carved base.

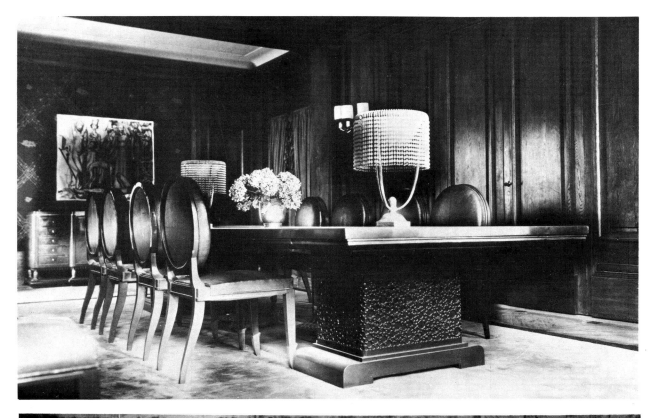

Berger Dining Room. 1924. Double pedestal table in solid wood with carved pebbling.

Astrakan Table. Circa 1926. Ref 1012 AR/1303 NR. Noteworthy because of the square pedestal supporting the slim ogee moulded top.

Salle a manger W...
table Ebene et marbre
argentier acier poli

Windburn. Circa 1925. Design for a dining room.

Rodier. Paris, 1929. One interesting innovation has been introduced: three juxtaposed square tables with Italianate leaves replace the large table in the centre of the room. When separated, they can be used as pedestal tables or as games tables. The classic macassar ebony table with a square pedestal thus becomes a 'standard' in Le Corbusier's sense of the term, but Ruhlmann retains the quality of his cabinet-work.

Lorcia table. 1930. 1510a NR. A very architectural table in bur amboina-wood for a salon. The feet are connected by an ogee crosspiece and four veneered cylindrical legs support the top. A variation on the Reuter table.

Axelson apartment. Decorated and furnished in 1929-30.

Rodier. Paris, 1931. The panelling, bookcase and
cylindrical columns integrate the decorative and
architectural elements.

Vizella pedestal table. 1929. Ref. 1268 NR. A
curious salon model with a lobed support and a
bombé base divided into four segments. The
table contains a number of drawers in the side.

Haardt. 1929. Salon with round games table and tripod chairs. The lamp shades are ostrich eggs.

Preceding pages: Office of Monsieur Schueller, Société l'Oréal. A circular room with rosewood panelling. The panelling incorporates a double coffered door with a silver bronze lock plate, 'horn of plenty' wall lamps and shades in metal. The rectangular table (1033 AR) has a double lyre base and is in rosewood. The green morocco top is rimmed with a silver bronze listel. The cabinet is also covered in green morocco, with fluting on the front.

Salon area for a Parisian collector. Circa 1930. The rational aesthetics of the leather and saddle morocco armchairs with their unusual support (ogee base, arms extending to form the rear legs) are all the more surprising in that a sketch of them appears in a sketchbook dated 1915.

Hôtel du Collectionneur, 1925. Dining room. The room is bathed in a restful half-light. Ruhlmann placed a number of silver-flecked bands of grey between the light grey ceiling and the red-brown walls. The large carpet is by Gaudissard. A bas relief panel by Janniot hangs above the portor marble fireplace. A tapestry by Voguet and a four-door cabinet can be seen in the background. A bust by Bourdelle stands between the windows opposite the fireplace. The long lyre-based table and the *chaises-gondoles* with carved backs are in American bur walnut.

Gonse. Paris, circa 1927. Two columns mark the
transition between the salon and the study.
Bookcase and a neo-classical Sanders desk in
rosewood in the corner. The atmosphere is light
and airy.

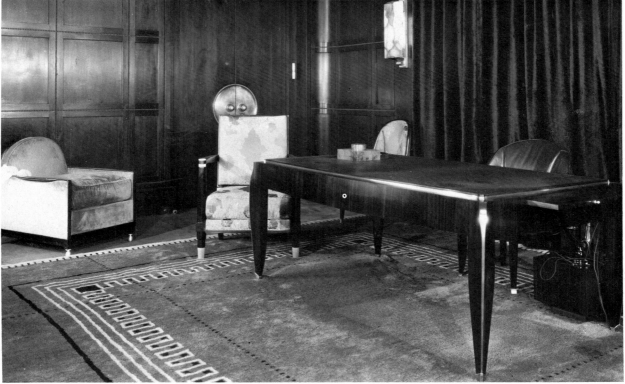

Bloch. 1927. The classic double lyre-based table as reworked by Ruhlmann: the top is in shagreen and the crosspiece-footrest forms an ogee. Examples were made in bur walnut and in amboina wood.

Ambassade 1925. The eclecticism of the chairs is somewhat surprising. Square rosewood panels on the walls.

Left: Tardieu desk. Circa 1930. The rosewood panelling harmonizes with the slightly lighter veneers on the hemispherical table. Photograph: Laure Albin-Guillot.

Haardt office in the Citroën works. 1929. A
classically functional desk (model BUP 1511 NR)
in oak treated with alkaline with matching lamp
stands in front of a 'mechanist' painting. The
comfortable chairs provide a contrast with the
deliberately bare room.

Fricotelle. 1931. The rounded desk emphasizes
the contrasts between the dark and light colours
in the room. The doors, panelling and bookcases
are contrasted with the plain pale colours of the
top of the walls and the ceiling.

Office. Circa 1925.
Engineer's office. Circa 1930. Reproduced in 'Oeuvres dernières de Ruhlmann', *Art et décoration*, January 1934.

Desk in solid macassar ebony with chrome bronze fittings. Salon des Artistes Décorateurs, 1926.

Haardt apartment, rue de Rivoli, Paris. The
two rooms are connected by the imposing
rosewood-panelled columns, which are both
decorative and structural. The study can be seen
in the background.

Home of Monsieur van Beuningen, Paris. Circa 1930. A variation of the black lacquer Tardieu desk (1517a NR), this time without pigeonholes, is set in an office incorporated into the apartment. The half columns set against the walls make this light and airy room look larger than it in fact is.

Dubly. 1927–29. Smoking room with games tables and bridge chairs. The walls are covered in
industrial lacquer squares forming a pattern of
rectangles and squares.

Dubly. Salon. In contrast with the sobriety of the smoking room, everything in the salon suggests a feminine atmosphere. The diamond-shaped motifs of the silk upholstery on the walls prevent the room from lapsing into a 'boudoir' style. The chairs and *bergères* are covered in velvet. The tripod table marks the centre of the large rose-pattern carpet.

Martellet.   Rothermere.

Rodier.

Halls and vestibules. Variations on decorative architecture.

Round Haardt poker table. 1929. Ref. 1266 NR. A
tripod table standing in front of a typically Art
Déco panel in engraved glass by Etablissements
Ruhlmann et Laurent.

Nicolle hall. Lille. The low cupola over the
square vestibule provides a theatrical setting for
this drinks cabinet. Concealed strip lighting in
the cornice.

Child's bedroom. 1924. Published in *Harmonies*, pl. 39.

Bedroom of Baronne Henri de Rothschild, Château de la Muette, 1924. Published in *Harmonies*, pl. 38.

Windburn. Circa 1925.

Lalou. Circa 1928. Design with marble walls. Ref. E. 176.

Lady's bedroom. 1927–28. A very light room
thanks to the contrast between the dark tones of
the macassar ebony and the light walls. Furnishings include the Soleil bed and the roll-top desk.

Marozeau. Before 1925. Ref 535 AR/501 NR. Double couch or bed. Single head, in bur amboina-wood with ivory beading. This model was inspired by the *méridiennes* of the Directoire period.

Soleil bed. 1923. Ref 542 AR/ 807 NR. A second example, also in macassar ebony, was commissioned in 1930 by the actress Jeanne Renouardt.

Design for the Château de la Muette, 1924. *Harmonies de Ruhlmann*, pl. 27.

Lalou bathroom. The walls are hung with fabric and not panelled with marble.

Bedroom. Circa 1925. (Second design, interior 4.)

Tardieu bed. 1929. Ref. 516 NR. Black lacquer
with a chromium-plated base, shown at the 1929
Salon des Artistes Décorateurs.

Rothermere bathroom. Circa 1925.   Martellet bathroom.

Rothermere bathroom. Circa 1925. The sliding door in the partition is flanked by marble columns, as is the interior of the impressively large bathroom. The plumbing has deliberately been left visible. The finest piece in this room – the Chinoise lacquered dressing-table by Dunand – was not installed until after Lord Rothermere's marriage to Miss Redhead, who acquired it in 1927.

Chamard bathroom. Engraved glass decorative
panel in the alcove. The projecting bath leaves
the plumbing visible.

Martellet bathroom. The bathroom as marble palace.

Ruhlmann's contribution to the theatre: he designed one theatre and one cinema, and the sets for a play and a film.

Théâtre de la Michodière. 1924–25. This small theatre near the Restaurant Drouant, which was also decorated by Ruhlmann and Boileau, opened on 16 November 1925 with *L'Infidèle éperdue*, a new play by Jacques Natanson starring Harry Baur and Valentine Tessier. The owner, Quinson, who was also director of the Palais Royal, decided in 1924 to commission Bruynell as architect and Ruhlmann as decorator. The latter submitted two designs. In the first, more architectural design, the auditorium was decorated with broad flutings. In the second, more classically Art Déco design, the walls were covered with flowers and leaves. Unable to choose between the two, Quinson settled for a compromise. The stage is flanked by fluted columns in old gold, with a bas-relief by Henri Navarre on the pediment. The auditorium is decorated with gilded flowers and arabesques. Fortunately, the period decorations have been preserved, but documents make one regret that the initial design was not used. Ref. *Le Théâtre et Comoedia illustré*, 15 January 1926.

Cinéma Marignan, Champs-Elysées. Circa 1928. The spatial problems posed by the cinema were very different from the classical problems of the proscenium theatre. Working with the architect Bruynell, Ruhlmann used pastiche elements to overcome the feeling of impersonality. The ceiling is decorated with staff cornices, and the balconies almost touch the forestage. The perspective effect is created by the four receding planes of the pediment, the fluted columns and the three curtains, the last of which masks the screen. The stage itself was designed for ballet and cabaret. The same gilded and patinated floral motifs are used on the walls, the curtains and the open-work pediment.

Christine, play by Paul Géraldy, 1932. In 1932, Ruhlmann was approached by the author who asked him to design the sets and props for his new play *Christine*. Archive photographs have survived, as have the maquettes which the decorator had carved in limewood before the full-size or outsize sets were made. The sets were scaled both to the stage and to the stature of the actors, Victor Francen and Mary Marquet. In her memoirs (*Ce que j'ose dire*, Ed. Jean Dullis, Paris, 1974), Mary Marquet recalls her surprise at seeing the imposing sets. The secret was kept until a week before the opening. The actors rehearsed on a bare stage, using whatever chairs came to hand, and were literally stunned when they saw the set. 'There was no ceiling, and the drapes disappeared into the flies. The set itself consisted simply of a desk measuring five metres by three, a gigantic armchair which took up half the stage and, on the other side, a club chair of Olympian proportions (the whole of Olympus could have sat on it).'

Christine. Play by Paul Géraldy, 1932. Géraldy's play required a set reduced to a bare minimum of boudoir and office areas. The stage of the Comédie Française is, however, extremely large (7 metres × 12.5), and Ruhlmann therefore had to cheat: 'His initial task was to scale the set to the large stage. . . the window was 7 metres high, the door 6 metres. . . The divan measured 3.8 metres by 1.7 metres and the desk 3.5 metres. That left the problem of the walls: only long drapes with subtle folds would create the desired effect. Monsieur Paul Rodier had a new fabric called 'Christine' woven. In daylight it looked like grey raw silk, but in the footlights it produced the required effect. Being a patron of the theatre, he generously donated the five hundred square metres of fabric needed for the set.' R. de Beauplan, *L'Illustration*, December 1932.

The façade of 27 rue de Lisbonne after the building was heightened in 1926. Ruhlmann's office was on the third floor. The showrooms were on the first and second floors.

THE
RUHLMANN
EMPIRE

Whereas most decorators of his generation had to subordinate their artistic ambitions to material constraints, Ruhlmann's decorating trade activities meant that from 1913 to 1933 he could devote his own financial resources to the most demanding of arts. He was fond of joking that 'I keep my interior design practice in the same way that some men keep dancers or racing stables.' He alone succeeded in simultaneously running his business competently and profitably and meeting the major expenditure involved in any luxury trade.

Early responsibilities. Emile Ruhlmann's family background and education shed some light on the singularity of his success and the human warmth that is still remembered by his former collaborators. Ruhlmann was proud of the fact that he was descended from a family of artisans and housepainters (and not, as is often thought, cabinet-makers) and was fond of reminding people that 'I was born into the building trade.'[1] His father, François Ruhlmann, was one of the old school and had no intention of letting his son study subjects that might lead him away from the career he had planned for him. As soon as he had completed his secondary education, he was set to work with his father's friend and associate 'Père' Bucher. For three years he worked on building sites, painting and lining

1 His mother's family, that of Septant, founded their business in Paris in 1827. His father, François Ruhlmann, was born at Marmoutier in 1847 and was apprenticed as a housepainter at Saverne in 1863. Wounded and taken prisoner in the 1870 war, he refused to stay in Prussian-occupied Alsace and left clandestinely in June 1871 with a fellow painter and friend named Bucher. He found employment with Monsieur Septant's contracting firm in 1872. In 1872 François Ruhlmann was naturalized, and in 1873 he married his employer's daughter, Valentine. The couple had three children, including one son, Jacques-Emile, who was born in Paris on 28 August 1879. When his father-in-law died, Ruhlmann gave the firm his own name. This explains why Emile Ruhlmann, 'Entrepreneur en peintures d'intérieur, dorure, miroiterie, vitraux, vitrerie, ravalements', had a letterhead reading 'Successeurs de François Ruhlmann père. Maison fondée en 1827' printed in 1913–14.

Brochure published in 1924.

ceilings, sharing the life of the workmen and storing up memories that were never to leave him, even when he had his own company.[2]

By 1901, Ruhlmann was helping his father and was responsible for contacts with customers and contractors. At the same time he established friendly relations with a number of student architects, including Henri Tauzin (whom he met at the Atelier Pascal) and Pierre Patout (with whom he did his military service).

The death of his father in February 1907 left him in charge of a prosperous business at the age of twenty-seven. Being ambitious, he tendered for building projects brought to his notice by his architect friends and supervised the work himself. He prospered, but secretly cherished the hope of making a career in interior design. It was at this point that he married Marguerite Seabrook and had furniture made for their apartment.[3] Stimulated by his first success and encouraged by such important figures as Charles Plumet, Frantz Jourdain and Tony Selmersheim, Ruhlmann exhibited wallpaper at the 1911 Salon des Artistes Décorateurs. The final decision was taken in 1912–1913, when he left the old family premises in the Marché Saint–Honoré and took over a building which faced onto two streets and allowed him to concentrate and separate his two areas of activity with a remarkable degree of success. At 10 rue de Maleville were the paint, wallpaper and mirror-work shops; at 27 rue de Lisbonne the interior design and furnishing agency.

The moment of decision: concentration or partnership? Ruhlmann's striking success at the 1913 Salon d'Automne and then the tragic interlude of the First World War encouraged him to become more organized and to adapt to the new situation. He therefore recruited the little team of architects and draughtsmen whose names figure in *Harmonies: Intérieurs de Ruhlmann*, a collection of interior designs published in 1924.

As can be seen from his sketchbooks, the war years were an intensively creative period for Ruhlmann, but they also marked a downturn in his industrial activity. As a result, he was able to run both his companies single-handed, but he realized that once peace returned he would either have to concentrate on one or other of his activities or form a partnership.

2 When he visited the Hôtel du Collectionneur site when work was still in progress, Georges Lefèvre found Ruhlmann at the centre of 'a compact group of masons, carpenters, electricians, gilders, glaziers, Italian marble-cutters and builders' mates', *L'Art vivant*, July 1925.
3 Although she had no official position in the firm, Marguerite Ruhlmann (1886–1957) was in part responsible for her husband's success. In 1933, she saw to it that the terms of his will relating to the winding up of the company were scrupulously observed. The following year, she organized the retrospective held in the Pavillon de Marsan with the help of Jacques Deroubaix. When she died, she left some of Ruhlmann's sketchbooks to the Musée des Arts Décoratifs. The building in the rue de Lisbonne was left to Alfred Porteneuve's son, while Jules Deroubaix inherited the archives which provided the documentation for the present study.

Giving up the family business in order to devote himself exclusively to design would have been a tactical error, and it would also have meant betraying his past. The only alternative was to find partners. Unpublished notes written in 1915 reveal his preoccupations. In them Ruhlmann discusses the possibility of forming a group of 'artistes décorateurs mobiliers' capable of financing joint workshops and sharing the profits and perhaps of setting up a training school (cabinet-making, upholstery, bronze lamp making) and a joint company for foreign sales and perhaps French sales. Ruhlmann was anxious to defend the common interests of artistes décorateurs 'against both the salon organizers and commercial manufacturers', to ensure better representation for them in the struggle against foreign competition and to intensify publicity for modern art in specialist journals.

It should not be forgotten that the International Exhibition which had been postponed because of the war was likely to take place in the near future. The prospect of the coming confrontation appears to have emphasized the need for concentration. Ruhlmann was well aware of the fact that the German Werkbund's formidable efficiency was based upon very close collaboration between artists and industrialists. Was he thinking of a partnership in which corporate interests would be predominant and which would allow the decorative artists to reduce the manufacturers to the status of sub-contractors?

He never thought of forming a true partnership with a competitor. The architect Louis Sue and the decorator André Mare had, however, done precisely that by setting up the Compagnie des Arts Français in 1919. Their partnership was based upon joint responsibility, and their designs were drawn up collectively. Sue et Mare accepted both the advantages and the disadvantages of having joint directors and managers. Ruhlmann was too much of an individualist to delegate any of his authority in that way. Confident of his own abilities, he opted for a novel solution which left him full decision-making powers as a designer and ensured him the finances required for his prestige projects. Together with his friend and fellow decorating contractor Pierre Laurent he set up a company known as REL (Ruhlmann et Laurent) in 1919. The company's organization and strategy are well worth analysis.

Rue de Maleville in about 1923.

Secrets of success. Finally delegating some of his powers, Ruhlmann made his partner a co-director. The premises at 10 rue de Maleville became the domain of Pierre Laurent. His company became the biggest renovation and house-painting business in Paris, employing five hundred people including thirty-five mirror cutters. Meanwhile, at 27 rue de Lisbonne the name REL went up, only to be replaced as early as 1921 by 'Ruhlmann Meubliers'.[4]

Of the six hundred people employed by the group, only one hundred worked for the *meublier-décorateur*, and there was no comparison between his turnover and the extraordinary profits being made by the building firm. It was, however, Ruhlmann's growing prestige and influential clientele which brought to the rue de Maleville commissions which no traditional firm could have hoped to receive: the restoration of many public buildings including the Mairie of the Fifth Arrondissement and that of Puteaux, the Chambre de Commerce and the *gare maritime* in Le Havre.

The artist made no secret of the fact that, without this cross-subsidization, he would never have succeeded.[5]

4 While designing a poster for the 1919 Salon d'Automne, at which the famous *Meuble au Char* was shown, Ruhlmann seems to have had certain hesitations as to what to call his firm. One sketch is headed: 'Salon d'Automne. Meubles précieux par Ruhlmann édités par la société "Ruhlmann et Laurent"', another: 'Ruhlmann. Salon d'Automne. Meubles précieux édités par les Etablissements Ruhlmann et Laurent'. He finally opted for the layout which showed his own name to best advantage:

RUHLMANN
Salon d'Automne
Meubles précieux
Edités par les Etablissements
RUHLMANN et LAURENT
27 rue de Lisbonne.

5 'Every piece of furniture I deliver costs me, on average, 20 to 25 per cent more than I receive for it. I go on creating furniture which loses me money and which does not make me a profit because, despite everything, I have faith in the future. I also have another business which makes a steady profit and covers the losses I make.' 'I am depressed. I have made a net loss of three hundred thousand francs in the last year.' Conversation reported by Thiebault-Sisson, *Mobilier et Décoration*, February 1924.

Ruhlmann's office. Like that made for the Maharajah of Indore, the Tardieu desk is in macassar ebony. This is not the only similarity in the furnishings: the modular bookcase and the Manqbéton chairs are identical. The two armchairs in the foreground were shown at the 1929 Salon des Artistes Décorateurs. The bareness of the light-coloured walls provides a contrast with the shiny black surfaces of the great lacquered doors with their chromium-plated 'shield' handles.

Ground floor of the Hôtel Ruhlmann, in 1923–24. The furniture is displayed in context, as though it were in a house. Set against the panelled walls and the pilasters, the furniture and objets d'art combine to create an atmosphere of discreet modernism.

Showroom in 1930. A carefully arranged display of Ruhlmann furniture and antique objets d'art –
silverware, paintings and sculptures – designed to show that old and new can be combined to their
mutual advantage. Photograph: Laure Albin-Guillot.

Letterhead designed by Ruhlmann.

27 rue de Lisbonne. The organization of Ruhlmann's interior design firm is typical of his constant desire for perfection. The original two-storey mansion was small and was used primarily for receiving clients. In 1926 , the building was heightened by Pierre Patout and an additional floor was used for displaying lighting and furniture. It also housed permanent exhibitions of contemporary ceramics, glass and sculpture. In accordance with Ruhlmann's desire to reconcile past and present, and his wish to make his saleroom look like the home of a collector, antique paintings were sometimes hung next to the modern furniture.

The sales organization was designed to convert occasional buyers into faithful clients, and was extremely personal. Draughtsmen from the drawing office were responsible for sales, and visitors had a wide range of options open to them: they could choose from the models on display, from the photographs in the *livre d'or*, or from the pattern books (sketches with the dimensions marked in) and could take furniture on approval. Ruhlmann himself often intervened to suggest to clients that they look at his new models.

The salesman's responsibilities were much greater than in traditional companies. Once an order had been taken, he took complete responsibility for it until the work was completed (some commissions could take two or three years to fulfil). He submitted plans and discussed them, costed the commission in collaboration with the technical director, and coordinated the work of the various tradesmen.

The fourth and fifth floors housed the administration and accounts offices of Ruhlmann et Laurent. These were headed by Vansype, a senior executive and Ruhlmann's brother-in-law. On the third floor, two double lacquered doors gave on to Ruhlmann's office, the nerve centre of the whole building. This large room was finally completed in 1929–30. Opposite the drawing boards stood a huge semicircular desk in macassar ebony. A similar table was ordered by the Maharajah of Indore.

Ruhlmann's closest collaborator was his nephew Alfred Porteneuve, who supervised the production of plans for interior design commissions and organized the programme for the group's participation in national and international exhibitions.

The drawing office, supervised by Francis Huet, was on the same floor. The beam across the office bore a quotation from Degas: 'To make something that lasts, we have to try to make it last for ever.'

Until 1924, the drawing office never employed more than ten people. Between 1924 and 1931 the number of draughtsmen varied from between twenty and twenty-five. After 1931, the depression obliged Ruhlmann to lay off staff, and no more than ten were employed.

The young draughtsmen (and one woman, Denise Nolin) were selected from among the best students at the Ecole Boulle, whose director André Frechet was a friend of Ruhlmann's, and were well aware that starting their careers with Ruhlmann was an opportunity not to be missed. Although relaxed and cheerful, the atmosphere in the drawing office was also hard-working. Parties were held when major projects had been completed to reward the team members for their unrelenting work.

Ruhlmann tended to regard his staff as his children, but he was very demanding and would tolerate neither delays nor amateurism. He paid them well (five or six francs per hour in 1924), and expected unfailing application in return.

Private views of the exhibitions were an enriching experience for both cabinet-makers and draughtsmen, who otherwise rarely came into contact with one another. On these occasions, Ruhlmann encouraged them to develop their critical judgment, to get to know one another and to realize that their specialist activities were in fact complementary.

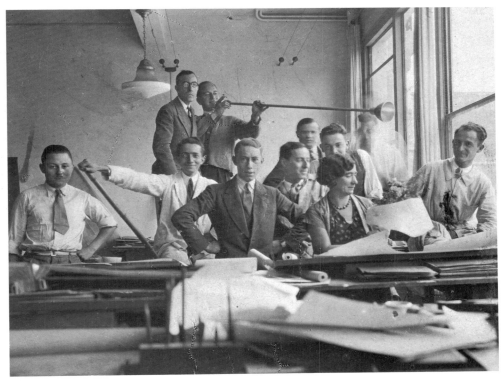

The drawing office in 1929–1930.

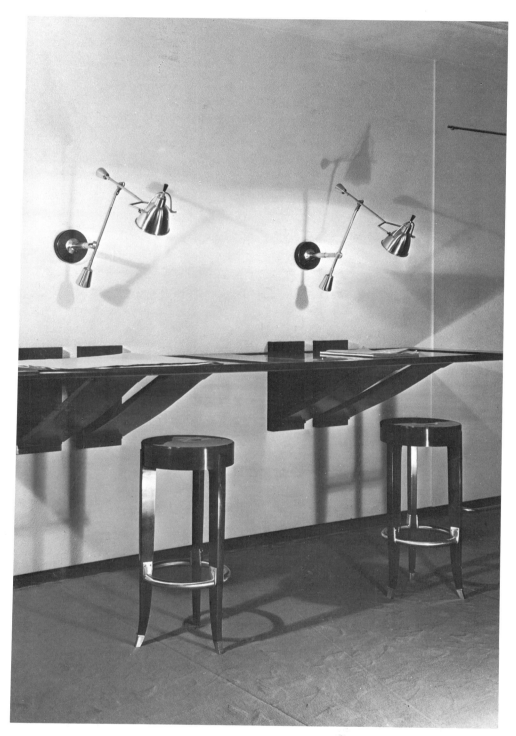

Ruhlmann's office, rue de Lisbonne. Circa 1931.
Like the main desk, the drawing-boards are lit
by functional lamps. The high Ducharne stools
are in macassar ebony veneer and chromium-
plated bronze.

Rue d'Ouessant. Contrary to the legend which arose because of his perfectionism, Ruhlmann was not a cabinet-maker and had no first-hand knowledge of the craft. This meant that, like many other Art Déco furniture-designers (only Jules Leleu and Léon Jallot had any practical experience of working with wood), he was dependent upon out-workers.

The only solution to this problem was to set up his own workshops. But in the early days that would have involved major investments for an uncertain return and meant overcoming numerous obstacles: finding raw materials and buying them in small quantities (and therefore at considerable expense), coordinating the work of various craftsmen. . . It would also have been difficult for a beginner to retain the loyalty of competent workmen and supervise their work.

Between 1913 and 1923 Ruhlmann was therefore content to have the furniture he designed made up for him in the Faubourg Saint-Antoine. His sub-contractors included Haentges-Frères (who appear to have made either the Elysée sideboard or the Yardley variation on it) and Fenot, his accredited supplier and a master craftsman who made most of Ruhlmann's early 'precious' pieces.

In 1919, the decorator acquired industrial premises between the rue d'Ouessant and the rue Pondichéry in the Fifteenth Arrondissement, intending to fit it out for his paint, upholstery, mirror and wallpaper departments. As yet, he had no plans for a cabinet-making shop. It was only in 1923 that his growing reputation as a furniture-designer and the scale of his participation in the Exposition des Arts Décoratifs persuaded him that he should recruit his own workforce. He asked Fenot to recruit between six and eight cabinet-makers in accordance with the age-old traditions of their craft. Every Monday, the cabinet-makers of the Faubourg Saint-Antoine would gather in the Cheval Blanc café, where masters and craftsmen would discuss terms of employment and payment. Ruhlmann was quite prepared to pay high wages to get the best hands.[6]

6 In 1925–1926, an experienced craftsman could earn at most 4.75f per hour. Fenot took men on at 5.25f, rising to 5.75f after four months if they worked satisfactorily during their trial period.

The cabinet-making shop was set up in a well-lit room on the third floor of the building in the rue d'Ouessant and was equipped with advanced machinery. Ruhlmann had no doubts on that score: 'It seems nonsensical to me wilfully to ignore mechanical tools. I work on the principle that nothing that can be done by machine should be done by hand. Modern furniture has little ornamentation and consists almost entirely of flat surfaces veneered with precious woods. Machines make it easier to do the preparatory work, to make the carcase.'

In 1927, major transformations gave the rue d'Ouessant its final shape. The mirror department, which employed thirty-five people, was transferred to the rue Vasco da Gama, near the Place Balard. At the same time, Pierre Patout added an extra storey to the building, reorganized it and installed two lifts. Ruhlmann's brother-in-law Geoffroy was appointed technical director. The caretaker and doorman, who struck terror into latecomers, was none other than Père Bucher, who had come to Paris with François Ruhlmann. The garage and paint store were on the ground floor. The firm's vehicles were fitted out for carrying delicate goods; the fittings were designed in Ruhlmann's own drawing office. On the first floor, four specialists worked in the lacquer shop, which had a fume-chamber for dyeing wood and special equipment for producing lacquered furniture. The modern technique of spraying furniture with a cellulose lacquer was also used.

The second floor housed the upholstery shop. Between ten and twelve people, including a cutter and a foreman, upholstered chairs which were made by outside contractors (cabinet-making and chair-making were two distinct trades). Some pieces, such as beds and divans, required the services of highly-qualified upholsterers. To take only one example: two specialists worked for a month on the bed exhibited in the luxury bedroom designed for the 1928 Salon des Artistes Décorateurs.

The cabinet-making shop was on the third floor. Designed by Fenot, it was run by Apicella. It employed twelve craftsmen, two apprentices and a machinist. In accordance with tradition, each cabinet-maker provided

Cartoon. In 1924 a banquet was organized in honour of the architect Boileau, with whom Ruhlmann had recently worked on the Restaurant Drouant. All Ruhlmann's collaborators appear in the cartoon, with Ruhlmann himself pushing his nephew Porteneuve. The caricatures are irreverent but show no sign of malice. From left to right: Porteneuve, Ruhlmann, Laurent, Rousseau, Mourey, Meysonnier, Le Même, Haranger, Lautelin, Bougenot, Pico, Boileau, Denise Nolin.

his own tools and was responsible for their maintenance. Each received a monthly bonus corresponding to one per cent of his salary. After 1928, this shop became known as 'Atelier A' and pieces produced in it were stamped with an 'A' on the back.

The fourth floor housed 'Atelier B', which was fitted out with ultra-modern tools and equipment. Avon, the foreman, was in charge of thirteen craftsmen and two machinists. Both shops had equipment for heating glues and lacquers.

The fifth floor, originally used as a storeroom for finished pieces or furniture returned from exhibitions, was transformed into a panelling shop which became increasingly important during the last years of the Ruhlmann empire.

A partially covered terrace on the sixth floor was used to store precious veneers and wood for making carcases under the supervision of Schlosser, a cabinet-maker who occasionally acted as a temporary foreman when required. He calculated the quantity of wood needed for each piece and issued it to the craftsmen. The foreman calculated the cost price and the time the job would take. The cabinet-makers themselves were not informed of his estimates. Waste and delay were not allowed; on the other hand, the fastest and most skilful workers were given productivity bonuses corresponding to the time they saved.

The clientele. Although it is not possible to list all Ruhlmann's customers, the archives and certificates of guarantee do give us a certain idea of who they were.

The Nicolle and Rodier families and the Rasson and Ducharne families represented the textile and silk industries respectively. The specialist trades were represented by Schueller, the owner of L'Oréal and, like Ruhlmann, an Alsatian; Miguet and Berger were timber merchants; Gautier a champagne merchant; Sools made hats.

A number of architects, not all of whom were his collaborators, asked Ruhlmann to furnish and sometimes to decorate their homes. They included Gonse, J. Bloch, Boileau, Patout, Marozeau and Arfvidson.

Clients from the world of fashion included Doucet, Caroline Reboux, Jane Regny, Fernande Cabanel, Madame Puiforcat, Madame Paquin, Yardley and Drouant. Others included leading industrialists like Voisins and Coty, fashionable actresses such as Jeanne Renouardt and Gabrielle Lorcia, bankers (Worms, de Rivaud and Rothschild), politicians (André Tardieu) and writers (Roger Martin du Gard, Colette and André Pascal).

The above list may give the impression that most of Ruhlmann's clients were Parisians. He did, however, also have fervent admirers in the

French provinces and abroad, the most famous being the young Maharajah of Indore. Other foreign clients included Miss Redhead, Lord Rothermere, the Comte de Vizella and Van Beuningen.[7]

Ruhlmann was not simply a tradesman who was paid for his services. People fought for the honour of being his client, even though his reputation was not based upon obtrusive advertising or society gossip. Ruhlmann did of course take part in collective exhibitions and held his own in the rue de Lisbonne. But he received few guests, and they were usually restricted to personal friends. His loyalty, his serious-minded approach to business and his talent inspired confidence in his clients, many of whom became his friends. He, in return, insisted on giving them satisfaction in every detail.[8]

Ruhlmann's prices may seem exorbitant, but present-day prices for rare pieces of furniture are far in excess of the sums originally invested. Compared with the expensive caprices of fashion, buying Ruhlmann furniture was in fact an excellent investment.[9]

7 Extravagance may have been the prerogative of a cosmopolitan minority, but average incomes in France did rise by thirty per cent in the twenties. Inflation had a stimulating effect on the decorative arts. Although it had been negative since the beginning of the century, the balance of payments was now positive: in 1928, exports of furniture earned 180 million francs, 70 million from Europe, 80 million from America, and 30 from the colonial empire.
8 During a visit to Tardieu, he noticed that the lacquer on a chair was flaking off. He took an immediate note of this: 'We will take back the chair and relacquer it. Better still, we will make a similar chair in rosewood, which will not flake. That would be the best solution.'
9 Reductions were made for potential or faithful customers. Exhibition pieces were sold in annual private sales, at prices reduced by 30 to 50 per cent. When he was hit by the depression, Ruhlmann was quite prepared to lose money to keep his employees working, as can be seen from the accounts for the Granet commission.
  In 1925 the *Meuble au Char* was sold for 50,000 francs. Five Citroën 5CV cars could have been bought for the same amount. But between May 1926 and March 1927, Josephine Baker bought clothes and stage costumes worth 235,000 francs from Paul Poiret.

E. J. RUHLMANN
MEUBLIER A PARIS
27, RUE DE LISBONNE

MODÈLE Nº _Lit (soleil)_ _807_   EXEMPLAIRE Nº _2_

Acquis par M _adame J. Renouardt_

2 rue Buzenval St Cloud (s.o.)

Exécuté dans mon atelier _B_

et achevé en _Juin 1930_

PARTICULARITÉS DE L'EXEMPLAIRE :

_Ebène macassar - finition cellulosique brillante -
plaqué soleil._

Cet exemplaire porte les signatures
et indications d'Atelier suivantes,
en bas et à gauche de la
face postérieure.

193

Certificate of guarantee. One of the two coupons
should have been deposited in the Musée des
Arts Décoratifs.

The end of the Ruhlmann empire. The world-wide economic recession led to a fall in orders and to a downturn in the building and decorating trades in 1932. Ruhlmann was less seriously affected than some of his colleagues, whose activities were compromised, and was able to devote a budget of 400,000 francs to the 'Rendez-vous de pêcheurs de truites', the largest stand at the 1932 Salon des Artistes Décorateurs.

But in 1933 he could no longer avoid laying off staff, both from the workshops, where overtime had already been abolished, and from his design agency. Hiding his own doubts, he told everyone of his plans to survive this difficult period. In August, he left for his house at Lyons-la-Forêt. He look tired and careworn, but there seemed to be no reason to suspect that he was leaving the rue de Lisbonne for the last time.

He knew, however, that he had not long to live, and drew up a detailed will. It was at this point that he took a crucial decision: his will stipulated that Ruhlmann et Laurent was to be wound up. Alfred Porteneuve was made responsible for liquidating the stock. Ruhlmann even went so far as to design his own tombstone in collaboration with Pierre Patout and to ask Janniot to sculpt an allegorical figure in black marble for it. The plinth is decorated with motifs designed by Ruhlmann for his furniture (locks, handles, *sabots* and ogee mouldings).

He died on 15 November 1933 at the age of fifty-four. The entire artistic world paid tribute to his memory at a funeral service held in the Oratoire du Louvre.[10]

After his death, everything happened very quickly. In the ensuing weeks the staff were all paid off, with the exception of a skeleton crew who filled outstanding orders and made preparations for the retrospective exhibition held in the Musée des Arts Décoratifs between October and December 1934.

Pierre Laurent retained his premises in the rue Maleville, but Ruhlmann's nephew had to leave 27 rue de Lisbonne: Ruhlmann refused to let the firm which bore his name outlive him. Porteneuve completed the outstanding furniture commissions, and then in June 1934 moved to 47 rue de Lisbonne. His uncle had left him a number of working drawings and had authorized him to reproduce a restricted number of pieces, each of which was to be marked 'modèle de Ruhlmann édité par Porteneuve'.

Ruhlmann had one other matter to settle before he died: he wanted to produce a sort of catalogue of all the furniture he had made. All the customers on his books received a letter dated 29 November 1933,

10 Founded by his former collaborators in 1980, the Association pour la commemoration de l'œuvre de Ruhlmann has had a plaque put up at 27 rue de Lisbonne. Its aim is to preserve the memory of the great designer. A medal struck by the Monnaie de Paris was issued by the association in 1982.

together with a numbered certificate. The letter made it quite clear that the counterfoils should be given to the library of the Ecole des Arts Décoratifs.[11]

Was this winding up of the company an expression of inordinate pride, or of a legitimate desire to live up to his reputation? He told his wife, who approved of his decision, that 'You have to know when to turn the page.'

True to his motto of 'Think big, think beautiful', and sensitive as he was to aesthetic changes, Ruhlmann would no doubt have succeeded in adapting his firm to the depression; anyone else would probably have failed.

An artist has no successors. Only his work remains.

11 Unfortunately, these documents, which would have represented a catalogue of Ruhlmann's work, seem to have been lost forever. It has not been possible to discover whether or not the counterfoils were in fact given to the Musée des Arts Décoratifs.

Lyons-la-Fôret. Madame Ruhlmann, dressed in white, appears in the centre. Ruhlmann can be seen in the foreground, half facing the camera, with Laurent behind him.

Janniot's monumental allegory in black marble
in the cemetery at Passy perpetuates the memory of an artist who lives on in his work.

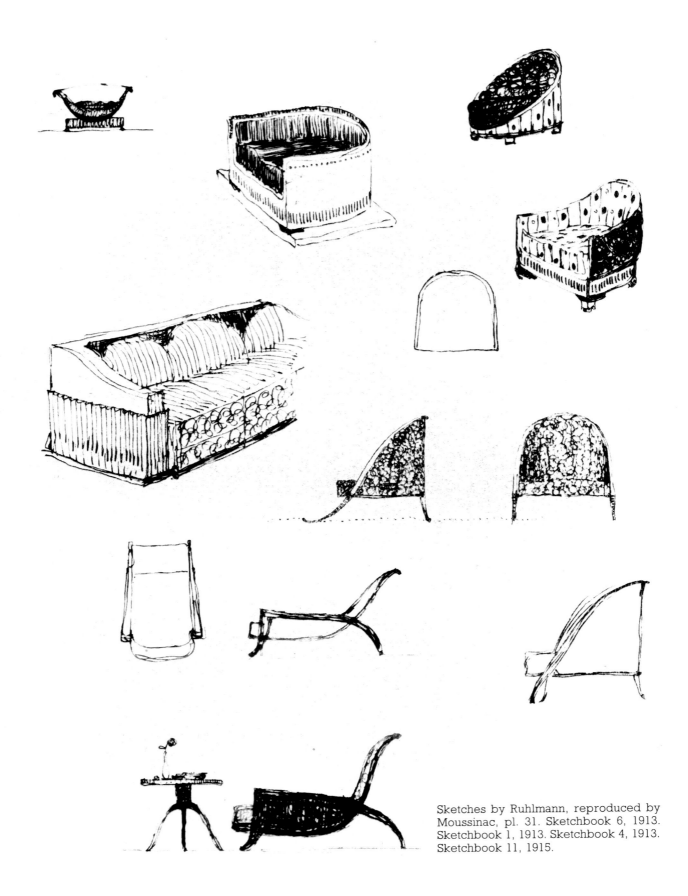

Sketches by Ruhlmann, reproduced by
Moussinac, pl. 31. Sketchbook 6, 1913.
Sketchbook 1, 1913. Sketchbook 4, 1913.
Sketchbook 11, 1915.

Office for the architect André Granet, Paris. This was one of the last major commissions undertaken by Ruhlmann. It was begun in 1932 and was completed by Porteneuve in 1934. A comparison of the estimates and the invoices shows that in times of economic crisis Ruhlmann was prepared to lose money to keep his employees at work. He could not have done so without his building firm.

The difference between the estimates and the invoices can be as much as 30 or even 50 per cent. In March 1932, the estimated cost of the macassar ebony pedestal table was 11,400 francs, in December 1933 an invoice was made out for 5,644 francs. The price of the leather armchairs fell from 12,400 francs to 6,000 francs in May 1933; that of the chairs for the salon from 13,700 francs to 8,000 francs (March 1933); and that of the rosewood panelling from 90,000 francs in January 1932 to 70,000 francs in March 1933. Ruhlmann states that all the figures represent a net loss.

Granet office. Paris, 1933. View towards the drawing-boards. The rosewood drawing-boards are attached to the panelling and are lit by chromium-plated adjustable lamps. The architects' stools are identical to those made for the Ducharne bar.

Granet desk. 1933. Ref. 1517 A NR. A unique piece, based on the Tardieu desk, in rosewood with a chromium-plated bronze base. This rectangular version is not really related to the prototype. Except for the adjustable lamp, the top is bare. The top extends a long way beyond the body of this knee-hole desk. The edge of the base is chromium plated.

Opposite
Granet office. Paris, 1933. 'Salon' area.

A cabinet-maker's log book. Jules Deroubaix, who worked for Ruhlmann as a cabinet-maker from 1926 to 1931, kept a record of the furniture he made, the hours he worked and the bonuses he received. The document is of considerable interest and is published here as a unique eye-witness account written by one of the last generation of cabinet-makers to be trained in accordance with traditional methods. It also provides a valuable picture of the financial difficulties facing the luxury industry between the wars.

It could take from two to five months to complete a single piece of furniture. In all the years he worked for Ruhlmann, Deroubaix completed only forty-three pieces.

The cabinet-maker worked a fifty-seven-hour week (including four hours on Saturday morning), nine hours of which were paid at double time rates. The hourly rate rose from 5.75f in 1926 to 8.75f in 1931. This represents an increase of 55 per cent, 15 per cent more than the national average over the same period.

1926 The first piece of furniture made by Deroubaix was the Jean Bloch desk (named after the person it was designed for) in American bur walnut. Ref 1025 (1506 NR).
This was followed by the Hanck divan, which was shown in the salon of the Hôtel du Collectionneur. Ref 527 (508 NR). Macassar ebony; chequered veneering picked out with ivory fillets.
Davène bookcase 2013 (235 NR). Macassar ebony with an ivory motif.
Elégant divan 514. The model dates from before 1920, but appears in the pattern book started in 1929 as model 503.
Hourly rates: 6.25f. Overtime could be paid at a rate of up to 12f when it was necessary to work on Sundays to finish an urgent commission.

1927 January: Jean Bloch desk, completed in February.
February: Elégant 1016 tripod table in Indian rosewood. Height: 50cm.
March–May. Two bookcases in macassar ebony for M. Zuccari and described in the pattern book as Grande Bibol Zuccari 2063 (2439 NR) on two scroll bases, length 2.9m and Petite Bibol Zuccari on a large central scroll base, length 1.25m 2064 (2362 NR).
June. The famous Cla-Cla reading-desk, so called because of the noise the mechanism makes. The second copy made in August 1928 in Cuban mahogany is in the Musée des Arts Décoratifs.
July. Two pedestal tables: Elégant 1016 and Sato 1038; also a Stèle table in macassar ebony.

July–August. Divan 527 from the Hôtel du Collectionneur, commissioned by M. Schueller, owner of L'Oréal and a friend of Ruhlmann. Made in American bur walnut, this was the first of a major series.
Sideboard table with leaves 1026 (1206 NR) in macassar ebony, but without the ivory dentil.
September–October. It took two months to make the large Duval 1511 (2300 NR) cabinet, made for Ruhlmann to keep his hats in (the interior is divided into cubical boxes). Macassar ebony, interior in bur elm. The doors are veneered with red tortoiseshell with diamond-shaped ivory fillets. Sold after the death of Madame Ruhlmann in 1958.
November. 1511 completed. Colette commode 2034 (1951 NR), designed for the novelist in the early twenties.
December. Jules Deroubaix began work on the Collectionneur desk 1063 (1541 NR) commissioned by the English collector Lord Rothermere. Writing cases and macassar ebony inkpots, designed as Christmas presents for Ruhlmann's best customers.

1928 January–February. Completion of the Colette commode and the Collectionneur desk.
Low table 1032 (1110 NR) in macassar ebony for Monsieur Dubonnet.
March–April. Deroubaix spends 478 hours on the dressing-table shown in the 'state' bedroom at the Salon des Artistes Décorateurs (1554, 1824 NR), which was sold for 36,400f. Legs in violet-wood, body lined with shagreen, interior in ebony macassar and ivory. A second

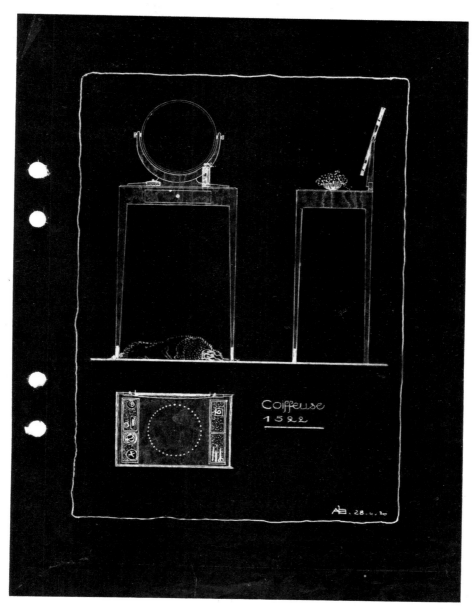

Morel dressing-table. 1:10 drawing, dated 1920.

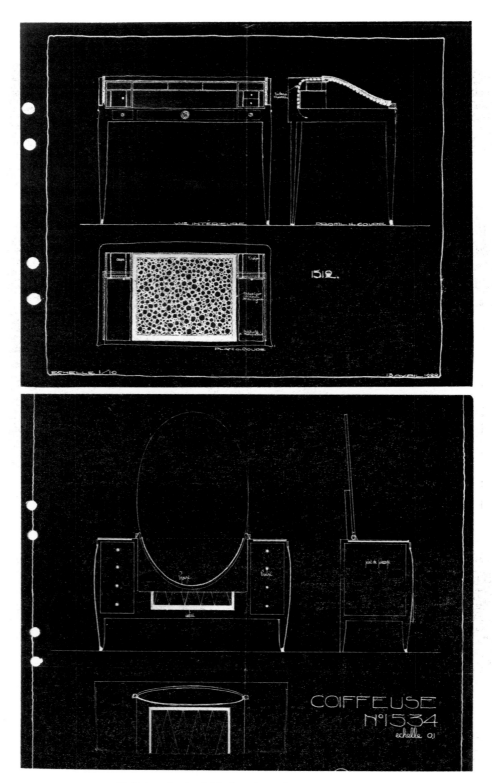

Roll-top desk. 1:10 drawing, dated April 1922.

Lassalle dressing-table with cheval-glass. 1:10 drawing.

version lined with snakeskin was made for Madame Ruhlmann. The original sketches appear in a sketchbook dated 1919.

May–July. With the help of a Belgian craftsman named J. Aerts, Jules Deroubaix works on the Wiener bookcase 2039 (2434 NR) and the Redhead cabinet 2014 (2128 NR). A total of 579 hours of work.

August–September. Another Collectionneur 1063 desk.

October–November. Deroubaix begins work on a long-term project: a particularly sumptuous version of the Bloch 1025 desk which was included in Maréchal Lyautey's office in the Exposition Coloniale. The desk is macassar ebony and took 815 hours of work. In 1929 the top was covered in shagreen and inlaid with twenty-seven metres of ivory fillets.

December. Preparation of three identical desks, which in Ruhlmann's terms was equivalent to mass production: the Crâne desk, which was catalogued in 1929 as No. 1603. This is a variant on the desk in the boudoir in the Hôtel du Collectionneur without the slatted top.

1929 January–February. Completion of the three Crâne desks. Deroubaix spent a total of 602 hours on these desks. This was a record, and he received a bonus of 519f.

February–March. Desk 1025 lined with shagreen. The desk measured 200 × 90cm and the process took 203 hours, broken down as follows: 31 hours to clean and blanch the 90 skins; 20 hours to cut them up; 152 hours to line the desk and inlay it with ivory. This represents a total of 1018 hours, including 815 hours of cabinet-work.

April. Nicolle 1076 (1264 NR) games table treated with Duco lacquer, which the workshop had recently begun to use. The job was completed in 180 hours and earned Deroubaix a bonus of 227.80f.

May–June–early July. Jules Deroubaix spends 471 hours on the Collectionneur 1063 (1541 NR) desk commissioned by Monsieur Schueller. American bur walnut.

Summer. Bedside table 1048 NR for the 'state' bedroom.

October–November. 229½ hours on a variation on the large Tardieu desk shown at the Salon des Artistes Décorateurs for Monsieur Hotschild, a South American client. Black lacquer, but without the letter files. This table became very well-known: other copies were made for Ruhlmann and for the Maharajah of Indore (macassar ebony).

December. Work begins on the fluted commode 2023 (1954 NR), an old model first shown in the Pavillon de Marsan in 1923. This version was in macassar ebony and was not finished until 1930: a total of 354½ hours. The front legs are in the *fuseau* style, which Ruhlmann was to

abandon. It will be recalled that it took more than a week to complete each leg.

1930 Completion of the large fluted commode. A large version of the Tardieu desk in light oak. Ref 1517A. Made between 20 January and 15 March: 334½ hours. Commissioned by Rodier.

April to June. With the help of an assistant Deroubaix executes the three concentric panels for the Soleil bed commmissioned by the actress Jeanne Renouardt. This was the second and final version of a model dating back to 1923. Deroubaix spent 252½ hours on it (this figure does not include the hours worked by his assistant) and was given a bonus for the speed and quality of his work. The cost price of the Soleil bed is known to have been 11,375f.

At the same time, Deroubaix works on dressing-table 1822, a variant on the model shown in the Hôtel du Collectionneur, with curved legs replacing the original *fuseau* model. Like the bed, the dressing-table is in macassar ebony and is lined with shagreen (14 skins, requiring 77 hours of preparation). During the summer Deroubaix mentions working on two 1002 bedside tables – a one-tier version of those shown in the 'state' bedroom of 1928.

September. Deroubaix works on a prototype for a chair in violet-wood (such work was normally done by outside chair makers): a variation on the Drouant restaurant chair known as Drouafine, for Monsieur Solinski (of Sools hats). The last three months of the year were devoted to a cheval-glass and a bed: cheval-glass 1517 (2441 NR) with three leaves in bur amboina-wood with ivory fillets; bed 894 NR in bur amboina-wood for the daughter of Ruhlmann's partner.

1931 The Nicolle games table 1076 (1264 NR) in bur amboina-wood commissioned by Monsieur van Beuningen took an exceptionally long time because the inner sides of the top were lined with shagreen. 218 hours were spent on the cabinet-work and 156 hours on the shagreen work: a total of 374 hours. Price: 8,600f. Deroubaix received a productivity bonus of 536.50f.

February–March. Rodier commission: office and pannelling.

April. Desk-counter (1401 NR) and conference table for the New York City Bank in the avenue des Champs-Elysées. Work continued on site through May.

June–August. First model of secretaire 1606A NR for Monsieur Axelson, after whom it was named. It took no less than 574 hours (almost three months) to make the desk and to face it with violet-wood: the veneer had to follow the curved, arched lines and bring out the architectural quality of the desk.

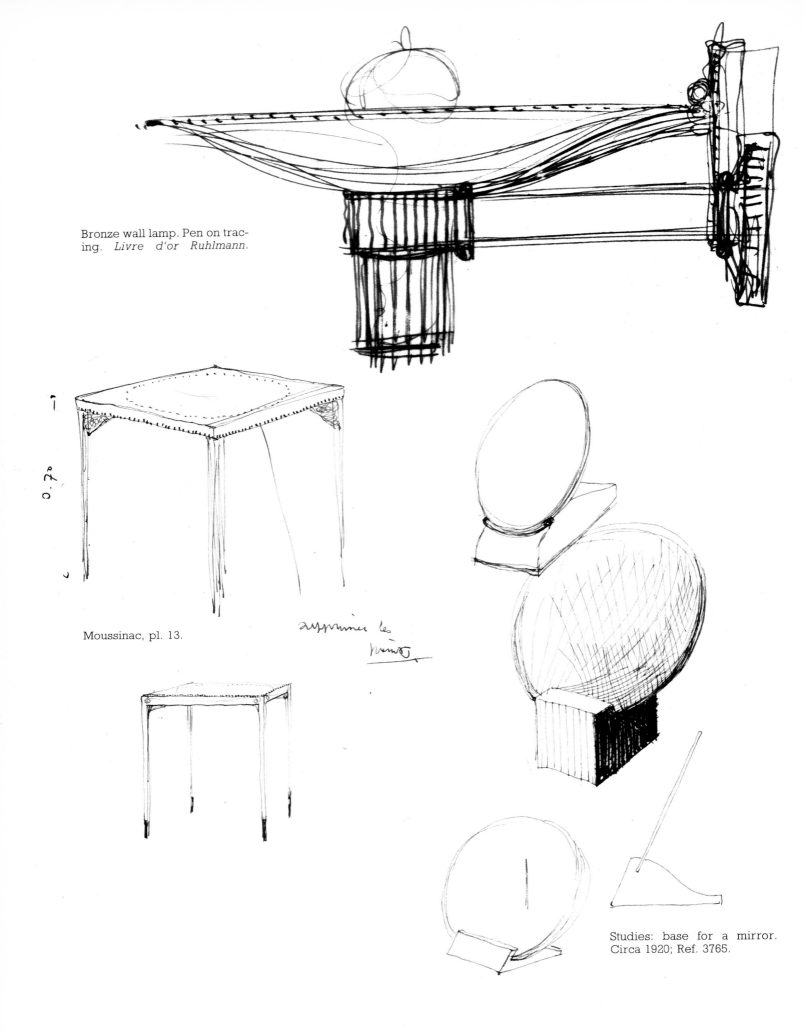

Bronze wall lamp. Pen on tracing. *Livre d'or Ruhlmann.*

Moussinac, pl. 13.

Studies: base for a mirror. Circa 1920; Ref. 3765.

The last piece of work carried out by Deroubaix in the rue d'Ouessant related to the study of the Maharajah of Indore: a long cabinet on a base with thirteen locking compartments (length 2.68m).

When he returned from his holidays in early October 1931, Deroubaix was transferred to the rue de Lisbonne by Ruhlmann. His knowledge of both cabinet-making and design meant that he could liaise between the drawing office and the workshops.

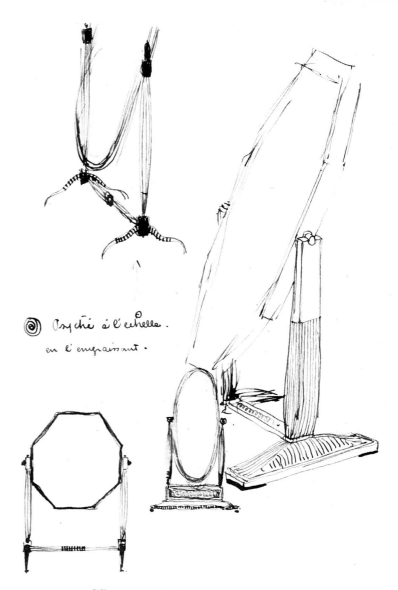

Mirrors and cheval-glasses. Sketches, 1917.

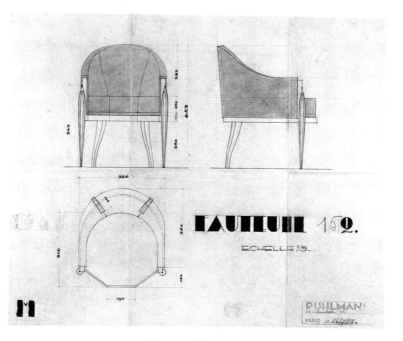

1:5 scale drawing with dimensions marked in by Plankaert, 1927.

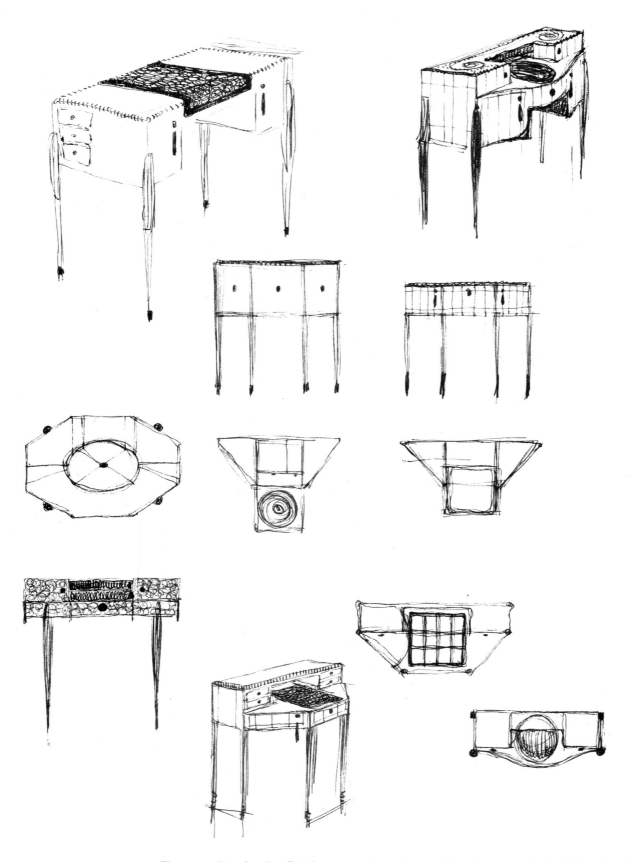

These studies for the Triplan secretaire, the two-tiered desk and the Cabanel kidney desk (Sketchbook 9, not reproduced in Moussinac) prove that Ruhlmann had developed the style used for his 'precious' furniture as early as 1915, even though the pieces in question were not executed until the early twenties. Hence the importance of being able to date the sketches, which Moussinac reproduces without dates.

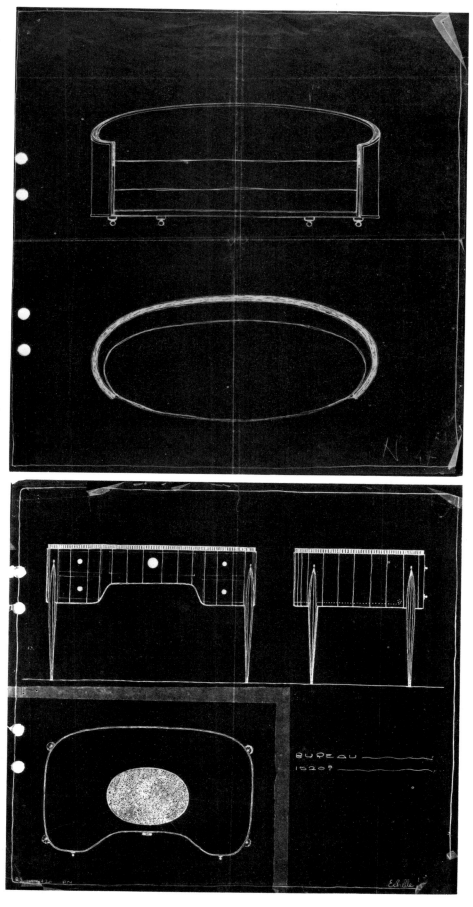

Oval *canapé*. 1:10 scale drawing.

1:10 scale drawing of the Cabanel
desk with dimensions marked.

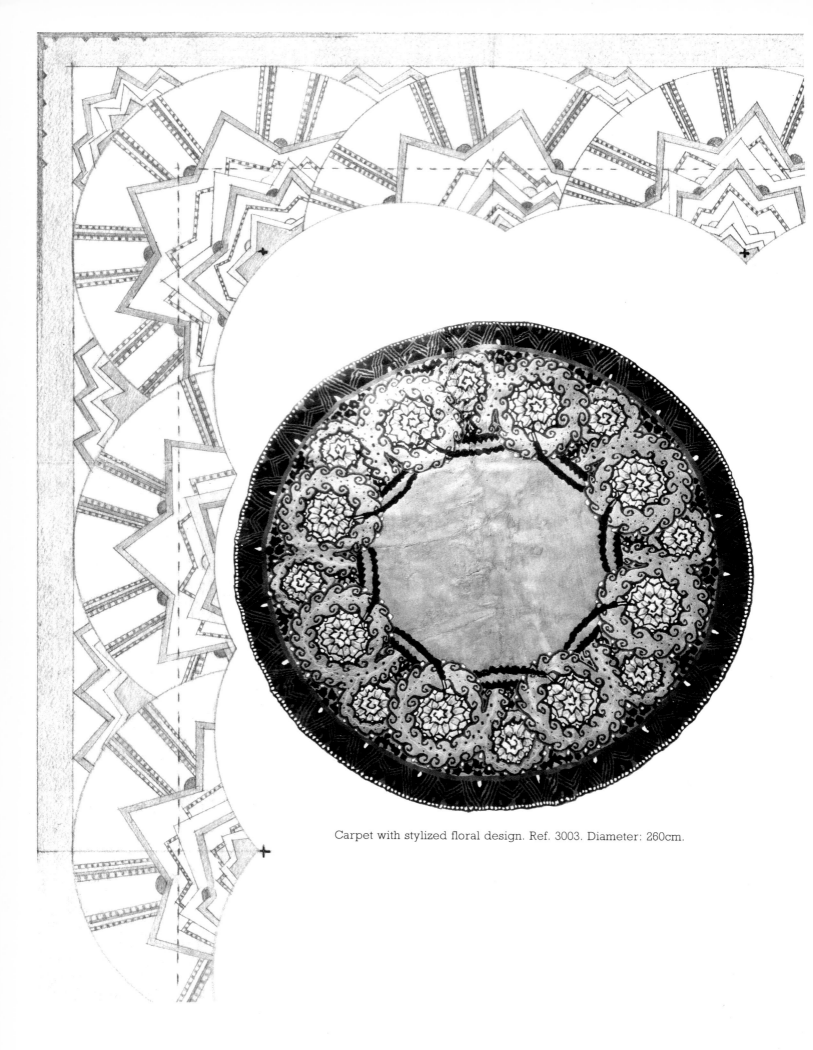

Carpet with stylized floral design. Ref. 3003. Diameter: 260cm.

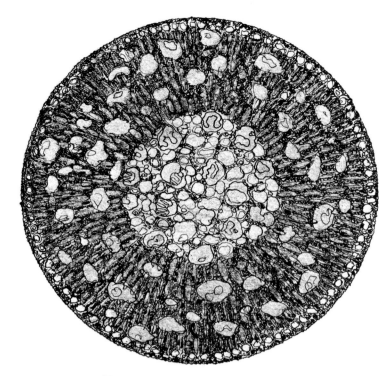

No reference. Diameter: 422cm.

Ref. 3001. Diameter: 280cm.

Carpets. Before 1925. Gouache studies and model. Ref. 3002. Diameter: 260cm.

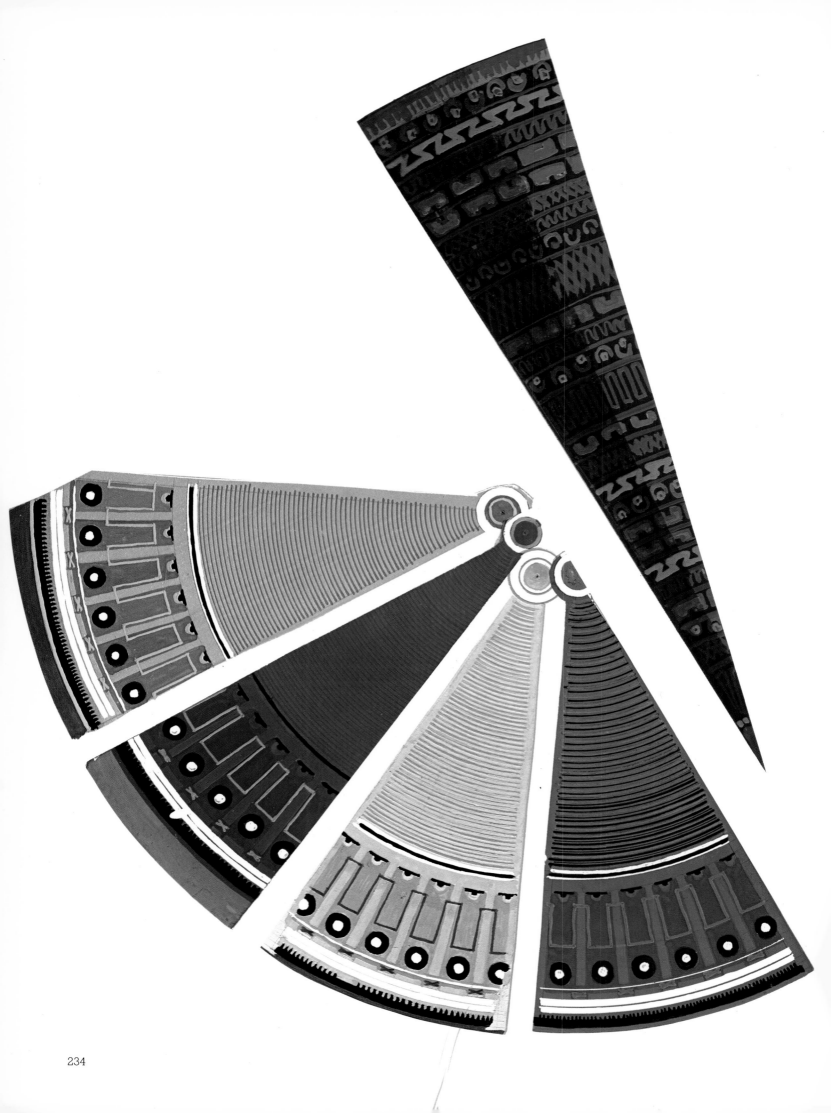

234

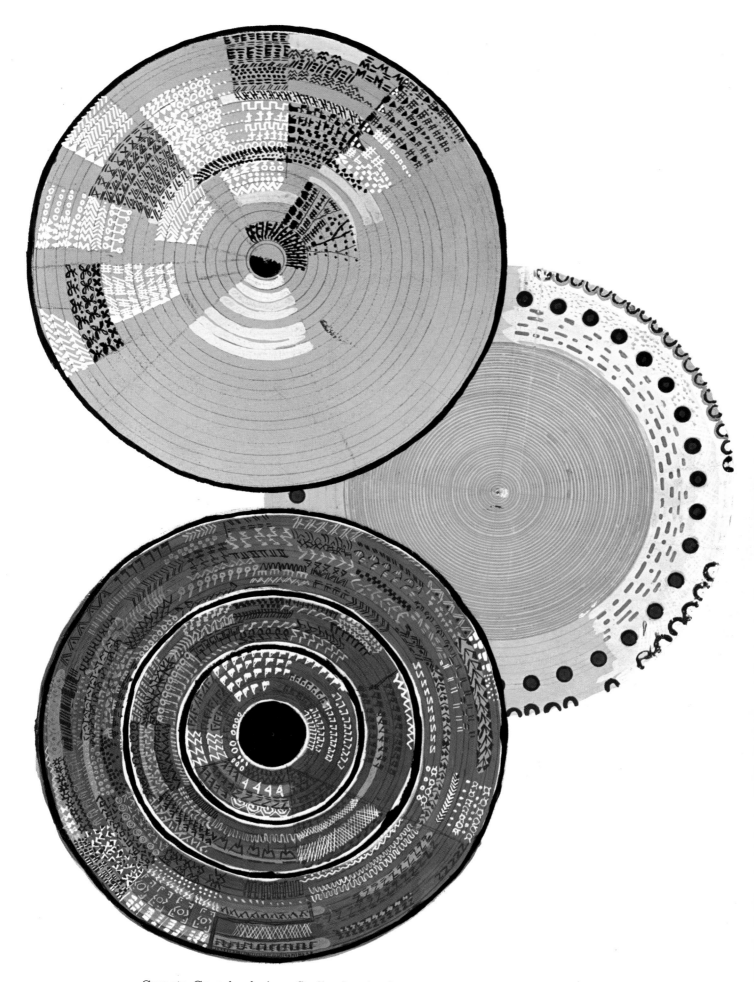

Carpets. Gouache designs. Studies for circular geometrical patterns.

Exclusive printed silks and cottons.

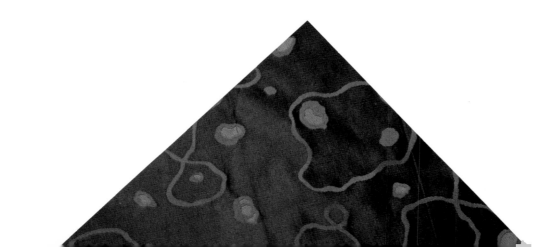

Wallpaper by Ruhlmann et Laurent. Circa 1920.

Sketch dated 1913 (Sketchbook 6). The carpet appears in the Ambassade 1925 office-library.

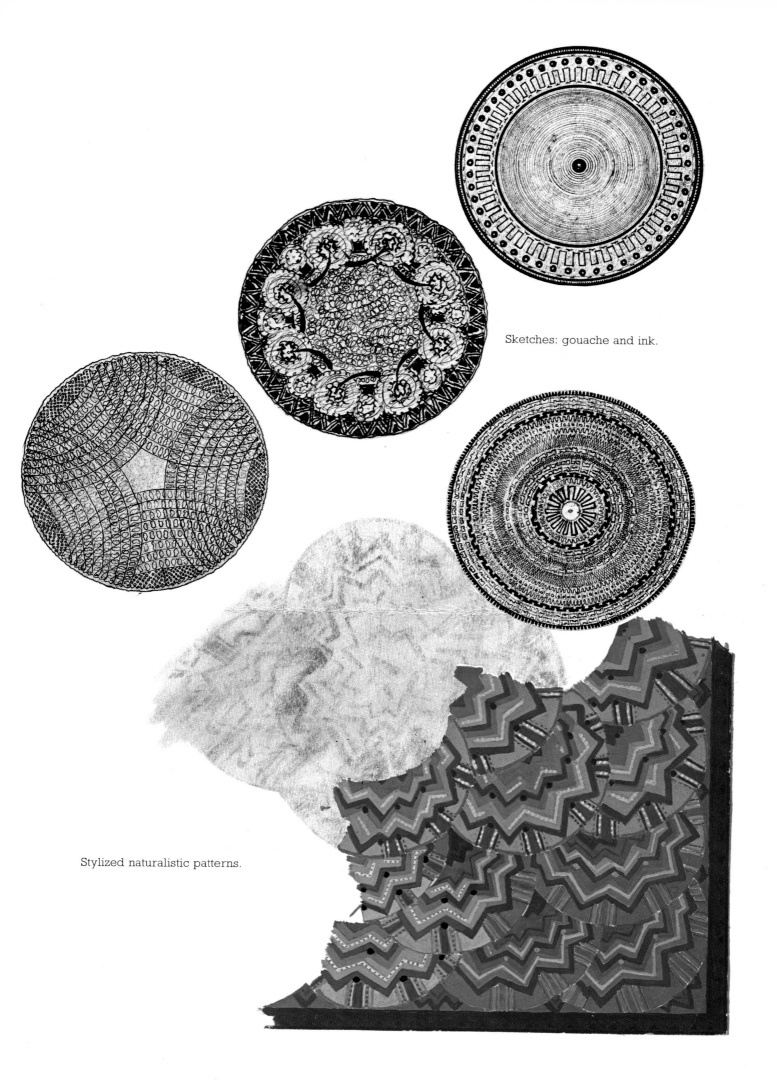

Sketches: gouache and ink.

Stylized naturalistic patterns.

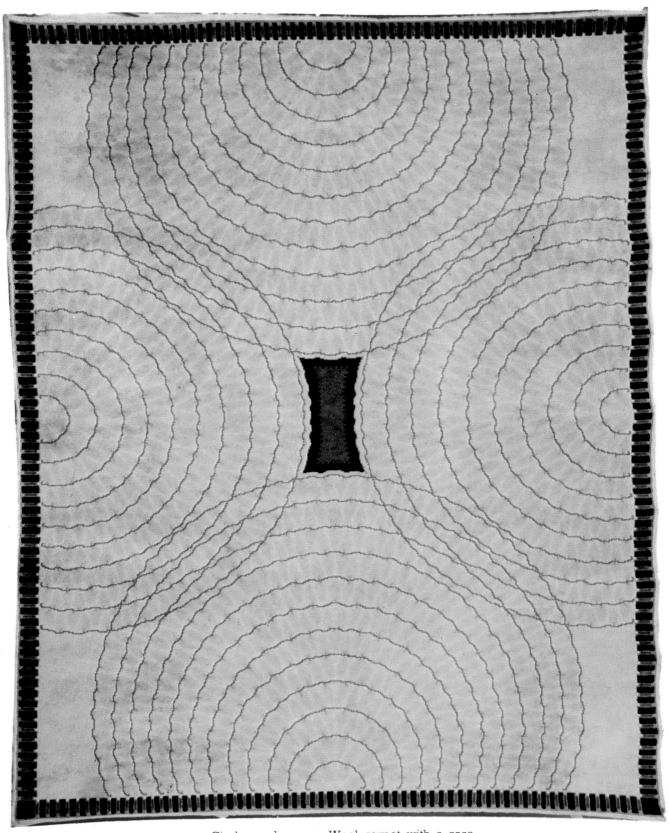

Circles and waves. Wool carpet with a rose
background. This model is by Stephany. Ref.
3180. 534 × 414cm.

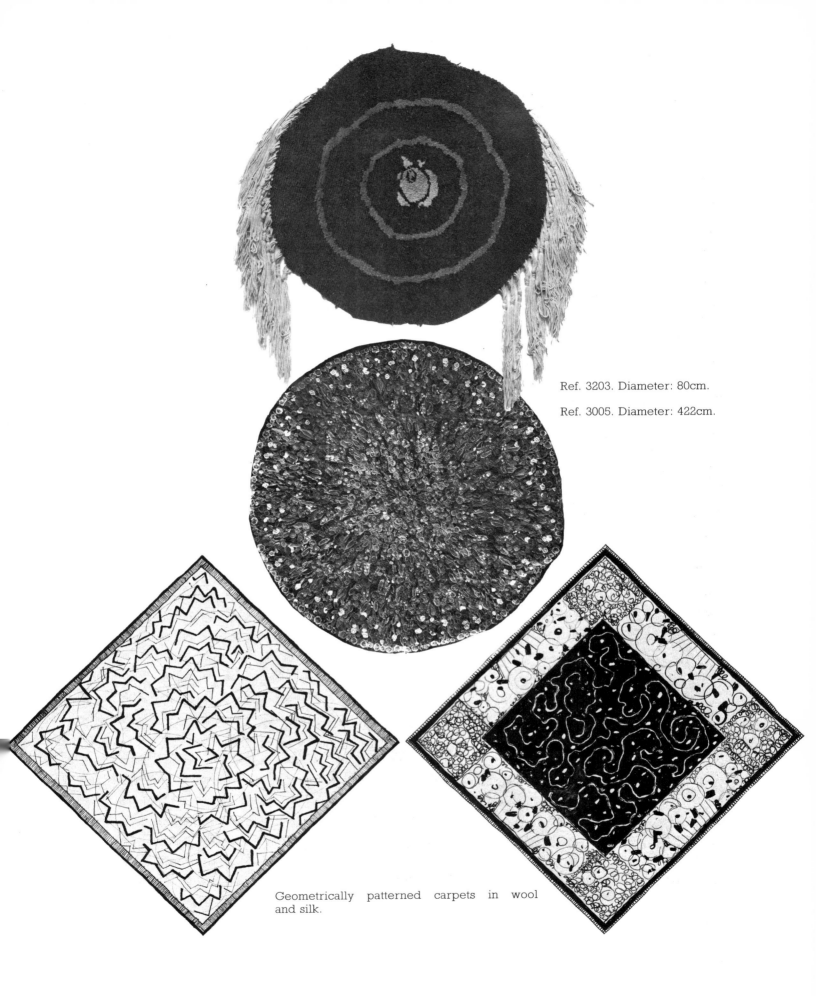

Ref. 3203. Diameter: 80cm.

Ref. 3005. Diameter: 422cm.

Geometrically patterned carpets in wool and silk.

Ref. 3107. 300 × 224cm.

Ref. 3027. 150 × 120cm.

Ref. 3015. 305 × 200cm.

Ref. 3056. 300 × 300cm.

Ref. 3055. 350 × 350cm.

Consoles.

Hôtel du Collectionneur. 1925. Fireplace in the music room. Ref. 3880A. The 'peachblossom' overmantle frames a painting by Jean Dupas.

Hôtel du Collectionneur. 1925. Fireplace in the boudoir. Ref. 3803 NR. This delicate fireplace in white marble is perfectly suited to the restricted space and intimate atmosphere of the boudoir. The hearth is concealed by a tapestry screen decorated with birds by Reboussin.

Colonnes fireplace. Circa 1925. Ref. 3814. The flat lintel is supported by two pairs of columns in 'peachblossom' marble. Burnished steel screen with sunburst pattern.

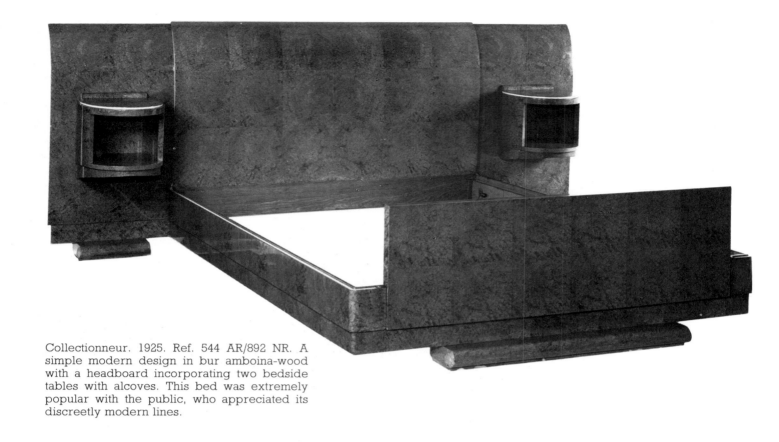

Collectionneur. 1925. Ref. 544 AR/892 NR. A
simple modern design in bur amboina-wood
with a headboard incorporating two bedside
tables with alcoves. This bed was extremely
popular with the public, who appreciated its
discreetly modern lines.

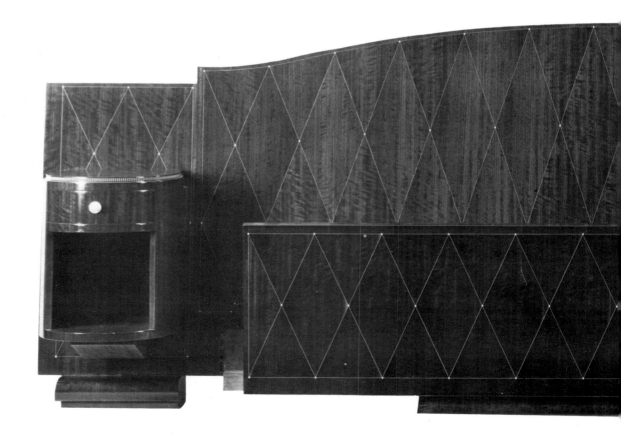

Dubly. 1930. Ref. 814 NR. Diamond-patterned rosewood veneer. The front panel is relieved by the effect of the scroll base.

Lit-corbeille. Salon des Artistes Décorateurs, 1928. Ref. 524 AR/808 NR. A variation on the model shown in the 'state' bedroom. Double laminated amboina-wood on tulipwood. Shown here without the satin upholstery.

Ruhlmann. Before 1925. Ref. 539 AR/512 NR. Single divan or bed in macassar ebony or rosewood with curved head and foot. This bed is ideally suited for use in a studio.

Sanders. Circa 1925. Ref. 537 AR/811 Nr. This imposingly large double bed (the headboard and side tables are 2.89 metres wide) in violet-wood inlaid with ivory divides into two single beds which slide apart.

Ducharne. Ref. 403 NR. Gilded wood, exclusive silk by François Ducharne. Matching armchairs.

Beauvais. 364 NR. An upright but comfortable model inspired by the Empire style.

Nicolle. Ref. 308 NR. Carved and gilded wood, with a slightly lobed back and hollowed out arms. Palmette motif on all four front legs. Matching armchairs.

Nicolle Rect. Ref. 368a NR. A straight-backed variation covered in petit-point tapestry. The two central legs have been removed.

Ducharne. Ref. 326 NR. Gilded wood with finely fluted legs and arched back. Matching armchairs.

Rothermere. Circa 1923. Ref 404 NR. This model evokes the nineteenth-century day-bed. All three external surfaces are veneered with macassar ebony.

Exposition Coloniale. Ref. 409a NR. A variation with three cushions designed for the office of Maréchal Lyautey.

Octogonal. Circa 1915–18. One of Ruhlmann's first *canapés*. Designed with severely architectural lines and covered with fabric.

Haardt. 1927. Ref. 408 NR. This model has flat armrests and is more severe than the Eléphant model.

Eléphant. Salon des Artistes Décorateurs, 1926. Ref. 409 NR. Made to match the Eléphant armchairs. Natural leather.

Fuseau-Facettes. Circa 1920–22. Ref. 152 NR. A low, rounded chair with seat base in three segments and tapering legs which typifies the refinements of Ruhlmann's 'feminine' style.

Défenses. Circa 1920. Ref. 177 NR. The arabesque of the arched back continues the line of the unusual slender, ribbed legs. Originally designed for a boudoir, this light chair was lacquered by Dunand to match the Chinoise dressing-table shown at the 1927 Salon des Artistes Décorateurs. Sketch dated 1913 (Sketchbook 4).

Salonicol. Circa 1925. Ref. 154 NR. A solemn neoclassical chair in gilded wood and tapestry designed for an admirer of the Empire style.

Octogonal Bas. Circa 1916–18. The back can be inscribed within an octagon. Padded armrests. The velvet is printed with black motifs and was designed in Ruhlmann's workshop.

Haut Ducharne. Circa 1928. Ref. 154 NR. Originally made in gilded wood (the chair shown here is in macassar ebony), this upholstered *causeuse* represents a happy marriage between wood and silk.

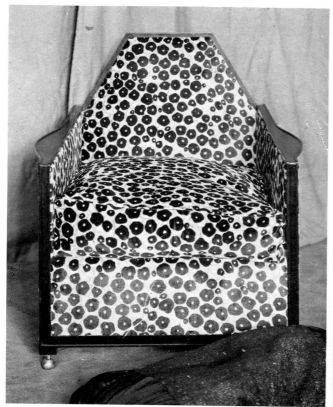

Byzantin. Circa 1913–15. Ref. 230 NR. A cuboid armchair which has the appearance of a sculpted throne.

Redhead Boudoir. Circa 1928. Ref. 227 NR. A comfortable *bergère*. Part of a suite including chairs and a *canapé*.

Coloniale. 1931. Ref. 52a. A variation on the Manqbéton model. The rear leg is extended to form a solid curved back.

Drouant. 1924. Ref. 1 NR. A comfortable, robust chair designed for the Restaurant Drouant. Oak chairs in the same design were made for the Ile de France.

Manqbéton. 1929. Ref. 52 NR. An original and unusual design. Its stability was improved when a second rear leg was added, giving a 'fishtail' effect.

Tivo. Circa 1918. Ref. 57 NR. Dressing-table chair with a low back. Macassar ebony or amaranth with a volute pattern and ivory *sabots*.

Cuillernic. Circa 1925. Ref. 92 NR. A classic
dining chair inspired by the *chaise-gondole*.
The upholstery of the back is particularly
comfortable.

Zucca. Circa 1925. Ref 90 NR. *Gondole* style in pear wood with a carved openwork back representing a vase.

Cabanel. 1922–23. Ref. 56 NR. Oval back with a thick leather cushion.

Tivo Cuir. Circa 1923. Ref. 56 NR. A leather version with a very low back which is more masculine than the original model.

Tauzin. 1913. Ref. 55 NR. Boudoir chair. Extremely elegant and original, although reminiscent of antiquity.

Palette. Circa 1925. Ref. 89 NR. One of the many variations on the *chaise-gondole*.

Citrodac. Circa 1927. Ref. 59 NR. Leather typist's chair designed for the Haardt offices.

Lanic. 1926–27. Ref. 25 NR. A thoroughbred salon chair designed for the Nicolle family.

Conseil. Circa 1929–30. Macassar and leather. The extremely comfortable upholstery, with two gussets, one sprung and the other unsprung, was adapted from a car seat.

De Becker. Circa 1925. Ref. 84 NR. Curved five-piece back in carved solid wood.

Bouillotte de Hanck. Circa 1927. Ref. 28 NR. The padded back and sprung upholstery were inspired by car seats.

Listel. Circa 1925. Ref. 49 NR. A 'tapissier' salon chair, with the side of the back reduced to a listel.

Cuellar. Circa 1919. Ref. 45 AR. The high rounded back recalls the Doucet *bergère*. Seat base in three segments, ivory *sabots*.

Ducharne Bergère. Circa 1925–27. Low version. The flat armrests are in gilded wood and are carved to look like strapwork.

Grand Canné. Circa 1930. Ref. 235 NR. The thick morocco cushions follow the curve of the cane back. There is also a smaller version known as the 'petit canné'.

Voltaire Bas. Circa 1923. Ref. 234 NR. The scroll armrests imitate the curve of the arched back.

Collectionneur Boudoir. A small cuboid *bergère* with very clean lines. Olive-shaped feet in gilded bronze.

Beauvais. 1925. Ref. 181 NR. The drum-shaped back, the *ajouré* verticals above the turned feet and the discreet use of bronze all recall Empire style. Music room in the Hôtel du Collectionneur.

Patron. Before 1920. Ref. 229 NR. A plain chair with classic lines designed for comfort.

Lelière. Circa 1925. Ref. 238 NR. A low chair with a rounded back and scroll armrests. The wooden frame is concealed by the tapestry cover which leaves only the vertical exposed.

Brouette. Circa 1920. Ref. 265 NR. The name (wheelbarrow) derives from the curved rear legs, which extend far beyond the line of the back.

Napoléon. 1925–26. Ref. 180 NR. The solemn character of the chair derives from earlier models, but the designer's personal touch is visible in the subtle relationship between the rounded forms and the angles.

Fricotelle. Circa 1930. 280 NR. A modern wing chair. At the back, the scroll base extends to form two spatulate segments.

Bergère à Skis. Circa 1930–32. Ref. 274 NR. The chromium-plated skis on which it is mounted allow this heavy chair to be moved. A handle on the back facilitates movement.

Repos du Pêcheur de Truites. Salon des Artistes Décorateurs 1932. Ref. 281 NR. The oak base which supports the chair is fitted with a handle allowing it to be tilted gently backwards.

Petit Haardt. Circa 1927. Ref. 275a NR. Larger versions of this comfortable cuboid chair were made under the name 'Grand Haardt'. Legs in lacquered beech.

Rendez-vous de Pêcheurs de Truites. Salon des Artistes Décorateurs 1932. Ref. 282 NR. A sober and functional small fireside chair.

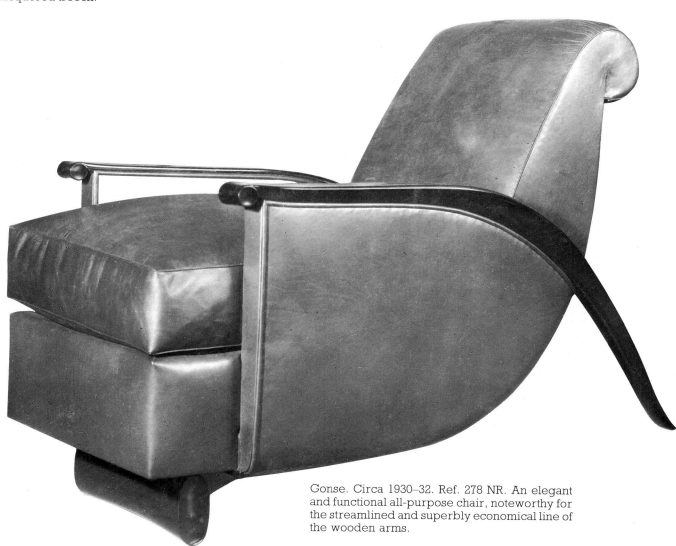

Gonse. Circa 1930–32. Ref. 278 NR. An elegant and functional all-purpose chair, noteworthy for the streamlined and superbly economical line of the wooden arms.

Retombante. 1916–18. Ref. 54 NR. Dressing-table chair covered in fur or velvet. The curve of the outline may not be logical, but it is extremely elegant.

Erard baby grand. Before 1925. Ref. 2056 AR/ 2492 NR. The novelty of this piano has more to do with the notion of suspending the pedals from a 'crossbow' than with the placing of the ribbed legs.

Leather window seat. Ref. 110 NR. A sober window seat which can also be used as a chest. Macassar ebony and morocco.

Pleyel baby grand. Salon des Artistes Décorateurs, 1929. Ref. 2496 NR. A modernized version in black lacquer and silver chrome of the waxed rosewood model of 1925. The broad fluting has disappeared. The pedal wires are concealed within a trapezoid shaft which looks like a central leg.

Eléphant. Ref. 276 NR. This model caused a sensation when it was exhibited in the 'collector's study' at the 1926 Salon des Artistes Décorateurs. 'The proportions of these enormous, fatherly monsters are so fine, and the colours are so well chosen, that they look light in spite of their weight.' G. Janneau.

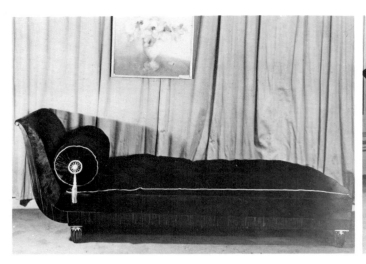

Marozeau. Circa 1920–22. Ref. 535 AR/501 NR. *Méridienne* with a raised headrest. Bur amboina-wood and ivory.

Elégant. Circa 1920. Ref 514 AR/503 NR. Day-bed with *gondole* head and foot. Violet-wood with pearls of ivory.

Méridienne. Ref. 353 NR. A late variation on the model created for Madame Ruhlmann and shown at the 1913 Salon des Artistes Décorateurs.

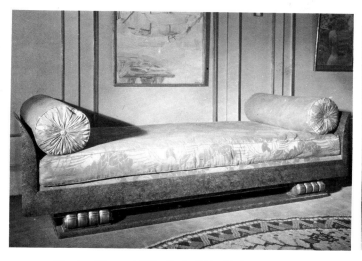

Bloch. Circa 1926. Ref. 553 AR/513 NR. The headrest is identical to that on the Méridienne, but the lower part is in bur amboina-wood. Recessed base with gilded bronze feet. Also made in violet-wood.

Ducharne. 1927. A unique model in Comblanchien limestone. The rounded head and foot are decorated with cocoons. The inscription on the bottom reads: 'Fait en 1927 pour Ducharne tisseur en soie, par Ruhlmann architecte, Le Bourgeois sculpteur.'

Bloch Bergère. Circa 1928. Ref. 226 NR. Note the subtlety of the link between the rounded seat base and the flat armrests. The ashtrays are detachable. The light-coloured leatherwork is designed for maximum comfort. A sketch of this chair, dated 1918, appears in Sketchbook 27.

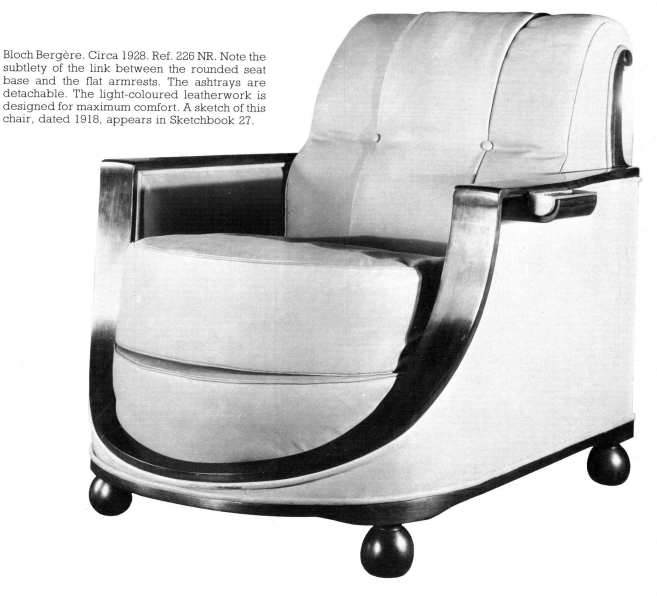

Crédit Foncier. Circa 1928. Chair in rosewood or macassar ebony.

Ledroua. 1924. Ref. 101 NR. Originally designed for the Restaurant Drouant and later used for the Chambre de Commerce (conference chamber).

Salonicol. Circa 1925. Ref. 184a NR. Midway between a chair and an armchair (the arched armrests are an extension of the front legs). Initially made in gilded wood.

Rodier. Circa 1925–27. Ref. 207 NR. Swivel chair in leather on a heavy base with four feet.

Tournmétal. 1926. Ref. 202 NR.
Swivel armchair made for the
'collector's study'. Salon des
Artistes Décorateurs 1926.

Salon des Artistes Décorateurs
1933. Ref. 156 NR. Lady's chair
in violet-wood and morocco.
This was the last chair made by
Ruhlmann.

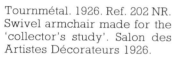

Maharajah. Salon des Artistes
Décorateurs 1929. Ref. 206 NR.
Armchair in leather and wood
with chrome base and swivel.

Francel. 1929. Ref. 205 NR. A
modernist chair in chrome and
leather which marks the final
end of the 'boudoir' style
dressing-table chair. Shown at
the 1930 Salon des Artistes
Décorateurs together with the
make-up table in glass, wood
and metal in the actress Jacqueline Francel's dressing-
room.

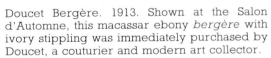
Doucet Bergère. 1913. Shown at the Salon d'Automne, this macassar ebony *bergère* with ivory stippling was immediately purchased by Doucet, a couturier and modern art collector.

Cla-Cla reading-desk. Circa 1926. Ref. 1070 AR/ 1260 NR. The lectern folds away vertically and can be adjusted by a rack mechanism. Made in rosewood, mahogany, macassar ebony, oak and lacquered limewood. The variety of woods used suggests something of the success of this ingenious creation.

Sideboard-bookcase in lacquered sheet steel executed by Subes.
Shown at the 1927 Salon des Artistes Décorateurs.

Secretaire. Salon des Artistes Décorateurs 1930. Ref. 1610 NR. Matches the chiffonier in the Jacqueline Francel dressing-room. The violet-wood veneer is laid in such a way as to reveal the shape of the frame. When opened, the leaf reveals a complex set of pigeonholes and drawers lined with doeskin.

Make-up cabinet. 1926–27. Ref. 1524 AR/2302 NR. A classic luxury piece. The case stands in front of a fluted column which appears to support it. Lock plate by Janniot.

Stelcavgo. Circa 1927. Ref. 1550 AR/2200 NR. Cabinet on a scroll base. Front veneered with ivory or with diamond patterned macassar ebony. A frieze of either rounded or fluted beading outlines the base and pediment.

Fontane chiffonier. 1923–24. Ref. 1533 AR/2232 NR. Bur amboina-wood. The curved line of the front legs is picked out in ivory. This double-doored chiffonier is surmounted by an ogee-moulded pediment. Musée des Arts Décoratifs.

Chiffonier with drawers. 1922. Ref. 1513 AR/2235 NR. The veneered amboina-wood body is supported by short *fuseaux à facettes* legs. Set of ten small drawers between the doors. Recessed pediment decorated with a volute and a palmette frieze in ivory. The drawer handles are also in ivory.

Etat Rect. 1920. Rectangular frame. Some versions were made with marquetry motifs; others were simply decorated with ivory fillets that divide the door into diamonds. The Museum of Modern Art, New York, has one of the former models.

Etat d'Angle. Corner cupboard. The only decoration is provided by the ivory diamond pattern on the veneer.

Etat d'Angle. 1916. Ref. 1521 AR/2233 NR. Corner cupboard with a *bombé* door decorated with a vase of flowers in ivory and ebony marquetry. This is the only time the motif appears in Ruhlmann's *oeuvre*. The example acquired by the State in 1922 is in amaranth, the one illustrated here in bur amboina-wood.

271

Bibol Trois Pleines. Circa 1923. Ref. 2035 AR/2334 NR. A cupboard or bookcase with three rosewood doors. The fluted frieze stresses its severity. Supported by two ribbed and ogee moulded pattens. Also made in amboina-wood.

Redhead silver-cabinet. Circa 1924. Ref. 2014 AR/2128 NR. A half-moon model supported by eight olive-shaped feet resting upon a flat five-sided base.

Redhead. Circa 1925. Ref. 2032 AR/2307 NR. Cupboard with two doors in Rio palisander veneer. The diamond pattern of the veneering is picked up by the silver lock plate. Recessed double scroll base.

Rasson sideboard. Salon des Artistes Décorateurs 1926. Ref. 2055 NR. A low sideboard with doors in bur amboina-wood, and a diamond pattern in ivory. The front legs are flush with the feet and are outlined with a silvered trim. The *sabots* are also silvered. Interior in Hungarian oak.

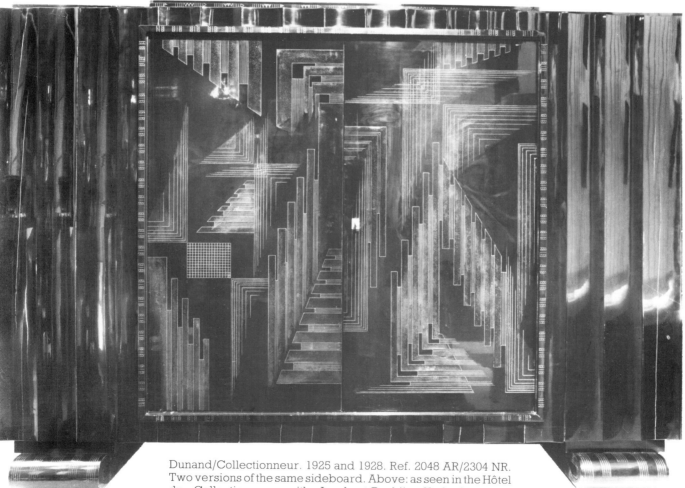

Dunand/Collectionneur. 1925 and 1928. Ref. 2048 AR/2304 NR. Two versions of the same sideboard. Above: as seen in the Hôtel du Collectionneur with Lambert-Rucki's *Hedgehog and Donkey*. Below: as shown in Barcelona in 1928 with the doors decorated with perspective geometrical motifs in silver on a black ground. The broad fluting on either side of the central panel gives this imposing sideboard an almost architectural appearance.

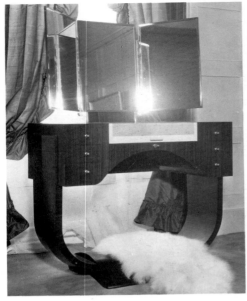

Van Beuningen. 1930. Ref 1828a NR. Macassar ebony. The side drawers are supported by a barrelled curve which narrows to form an ogee moulded base. The central drawer is partly covered by the ivory and shagreen apron. Unlike the Redhead (1828 NR) dressing-table, where the round mirror is set in an arc, this model has a mirror with three rectangular leaves.

Rendez-vous de Pêcheurs de Truites. Salon des Artistes Décorateurs, 1932. Ref. 2874 NR. Typical of the return to simplicity, this solid cherry-wood table uses techniques associated with joinery rather than cabinet-making. It can be used either as a dressing-table or as a writing desk: the mirror folds down to form a writing platform.

Redhead. 1930. Ref. 1828 NR.

Lassalle. Circa 1925. Ref. 1534 AR/1949 NR. An oval cheval-glass set in rosewood or macassar ebony with an ivory rim with two sets of drawers, one on either side of the shagreen table. The Lambiotte model is similar but has eight drawers instead of six.

Vasque-tapis. Circa 1920. Ref. 1531 AR. A masterpiece of *ébénisterie*. This dressing-table in macassar ebony combines sculpture (the vase surmounting the ogee base) and marquetry (ebony and ivory with a pebbled motif). Two turned columns support the ivory-stippled top. Two small drawers are concealed in the top.

Chinoise. Circa 1922–24. Ref. 1538 AR/1827 NR. A simple table built on principles derived from joinery. The only indication that this is a dressing-table is the circular swing mirror in a frame of white-leaded oak.

Berkocoiff. 1924. Ref. 1528 AR/1821 NR. Designed for Madame Berkowitz, this dressing-table has two cabinets with doors and three side drawers. The doeskin cover overlaps and conceals the front drawer. Chrome-mounted mirror on a lyre-shaped mount.

Dressing-table from the 'state bedroom'. 1928. Ref. 1554 AR/1824 NR. A unique piece. The top is cut away at the centre and is supported by tapering legs veneered horizontally with violet-wood. The body is covered with grey shagreen and the top slides aside to reveal two coffer-drawers. The mirror folds down to transform this dressing-table into a writing desk. Interior lined with macassar ebony; the *sabots* and listel are chromium-plated.

Dubly. 1929–30. Ref. 1819 NR. This oval dressing-table is supported by rectangular legs which taper as they meet the rounded drawers. Large fixed mirror in a mount of wood and metal. The combination of amboina-wood and ivory and shagreen marquetry is unusual for this late date.

Chinoise Laquée. Salon des Artistes Décorateurs 1927. Ref. 1538 AR/1827 NR. Abstract eggshell decorations by Jean Dunand. The matching chair, with feet tapering to arched 'tusks', was also lacquered by Dunand.

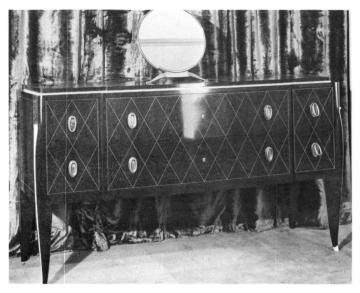

Lassalle. Hôtel du Collectionneur 1925. Ref. 2031 AR/1953
NR. American bur walnut. The ivory diamond pattern
emphasizes the lines of the central panel but conceals the
drawers. The ivory trim broadens into a volute and
emphasizes the curve of the front legs.

Redhead. Circa 1925. Ref. 2003 AR/1952 NR. Commode
with curved legs. The volute of the ivory trim emphasizes
their angular positioning. Nine drawers with silver bronze
handles.

Hussarde. Ref. 2069 AR/1955 NR. Shown in the 'state'
bedroom in the 1928 Salon des Artistes Décorateurs. The
bur amboina-wood veneer masks the crosspieces. The
three large drawers in the centre stand out slightly and are
flanked by six small drawers. Gilt-bronze handles.

Colette. Circa 1923. Ref. 2034 AR/1951 NR. Designed for the novelist, this commode was originally made in mahogany. Two drawers without crosspieces. Examples were made in a variety of precious veneers: macassar ebony, amboina-wood, amaranth and bur ash. The 'Grande Colette' version has six drawers. In later models, ivory replaces the silvered bronze of the ring pulls and *sabots*.

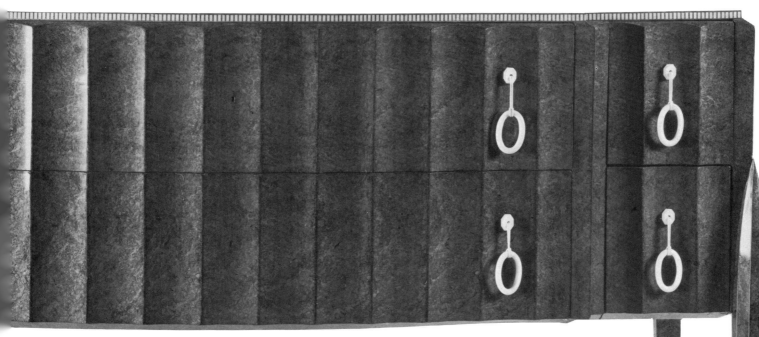

Grande Cannelée à Redents. 1923. A set of six large drawers without crosspieces on *fuseau à facettes* legs. This model is in bur amboina-wood; the first version shown at the Pavillon de Marsan was in macassar ebony. The veneering follows the line of the fluting of the frame and emphasizes the lines of the central panels. Drawer pulls in ivory with silk cords.

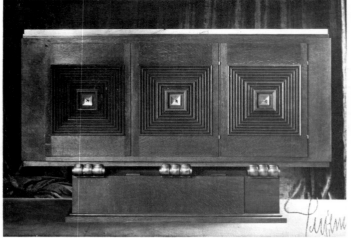

Geoffroy. 1931. Ref. 2135 NR. First shown at the Exposition Coloniale. The base is set back and is separated from the body by three large motifs in bronze. The doors, in rosewood or oak, are decorated with mouldings forming squares which converge around the locks.

Ducharne sideboard. Circa 1923. (No reference.) A unique model. The curious front, which is completely covered in floral motifs, recalls some Art Déco silks.

Berger silver-cabinet. 1923. Ref. 2028 AR/2132 NR. Cabinet in rosewood supported by bronze feet on a base.

Worms silver-cabinet. Circa 1923–24. Ref. 2028 AR/2132 NR. The reference is the same as that for the Berger model, but there are considerable differences between the two. The Worms version has two central wooden doors, or, in later versions, glass doors.

Demi-ventre. 1919. Ref. 2005 AR/2117 NR. Rosewood or mahogany. A half-moon-shaped silver-cabinet with two convex doors and a drawer surmounted by an alcove. Both versions, one inlaid with ivory, the other carved, have classic Art Déco floral motifs.

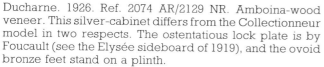

Ducharne. 1926. Ref. 2074 AR/2129 NR. Amboina-wood veneer. This silver-cabinet differs from the Collectionneur model in two respects. The ostentatious lock plate is by Foucault (see the Elysée sideboard of 1919), and the ovoid bronze feet stand on a plinth.

Van Beuningen. 1931. Ref. 2136 NR. A functional version of the silver-cabinet. The continuous horizontal violet-wood veneer conceals the doors and drawers, and represents a triumph of cabinet-making. The double scroll base contains drawers for storage.

Rendez-vous de Pêcheurs de Truites. Salon des Artistes Décorateurs, 1932. Ref. 2137. A long sideboard in solid cherry-wood which provides a wide range of storage space. The chromium-plated drawer handles and the inlaid lock plates are especially noteworthy. The latter are surrounded by concentric mouldings. A unique model.

Tiroirs-laque. 1930. Ref. 1956. A perfect example of a multi-purpose piece in black lacquered limewood which shows the evolution of Ruhlmann's style. The architectural lines are impeccably clean. The recessed base contains drawers for storage. The draw handles and listel are chromium-plated to match the industrial lacquer.

Rothschild Bonheur-du-jour. Circa 1920. Ref. 1523 AR/2201 NR. This small cabinet in amaranth or macassar ebony has a projecting door and stands upon tapering legs with a square entablature.

Telescope table. Circa 1931. Ref. 1047 NR. A functional model which is representative of Ruhlmann's desire to combine wood and metal. This small table is in mahogany. The adjustable support stands upon a lyre-shaped base and is in chromium-plated or gilded metal.

Coffret d'Or. Circa 1928. Ref. 1502 AR. A delicate *entre-deux* piece on tapering legs. The use of gold leaf on the carved wood provides a sculptured style of decoration which was soon abandoned by Ruhlmann.

Chevet Rose. Circa 1924. Ref. 1066 AR/1004 NR. An oval bedside table in amboina-wood with a recessed top ringed with ivory beading. The curve of the angled legs is emphasized by the ivory trim. Three drawers.

Chevet Rose. Circa 1927. Ref. 1066 AR/1004 NR. Rosewood. The alcove and drawer are in amboina-wood. Curved legs with an ivory trim. A variation on the three-drawer model.

Décorateurs. 1929. Ref. 1048 NR. A modernist side-table or bedside table in chrome and lacquered wood. One of the leafs is immobile. Used as a bedside table with the Tardieu bed.

D'Estainville. Circa 1930. Ref. 1055 NR. A narrow oval body in amboina-wood on an ogee base. The top is lined with shagreen and is streamlined like an aircraft wing.

Coffret Soie. Circa 1918. Ref. 1030 AR. One of Ruhlmann's earliest models. His liking for refined detail and his sense of harmonious proportion are instantly recognizable.

Sonnenfield. Circa 1929. Ref. 1007 NR. An asymmetrical tripod. The bookcase niche stands upon two half-moon drawers.

Ducharne. Circa 1925. Ref. 1080 AR/1005 NR. Oval bedside table with a recess surrounded by an ivory and ebony dentil.

Ducharne d'Or. 1929. Ref. 1113 NR. The original model had a support in gilded bronze to match the gilded wood furniture in the salon. The later versions in violet-wood or macassar ebony are masterpieces of cabinet-making.

Colonne. Circa 1929. Ref. 1142 NR. A tall round pedestal table with the support tapering to four pattens decorated with carved bronze. The circular top is veneered in macassar ebony and is ringed by a metal listel.

Calice. Before 1920. Ref. 1004 AR. This model seems almost to recall the floral naturalism of the School of Nancy. Drawing dated 1919 (Sketchbook 28).

Cabanel Basse-Boule. 1918–19. Ref. 1110 AR/1032 NR. Four ribbed balls set into a rectangular plinth support a thick top with a geometrical pattern in ivory. The top may be either solid or veneered. Also made in rosewood and macassar ebony (sometimes with the top lined with shagreen), in oak and in lacquered limewood.

Dorique or Pompéien. 1913. Ref. 1002 AR/1109 NR. This cubist-inspired low table magisterially combines form and volume: square base, polygonal support and octagonal top. This model in red lacquer was made for C. Devambez in 1913.

Araignée. Circa 1918–20. Ref. 1018 AR/1220 NR. The name ('spider') derives from the slender legs supporting the undertier. The amboina-wood or macassar ebony 'sun' veneer on the square top is decorated with a circle of ivory pearls. The Maeght variation has an additional folding tier.

Bernstein. Circa 1920. (No reference.) A variation on the Araignée model. The square undertier is supported by four legs; the octagonal top is picked out by an ivory dentil.

Colonnettes. 1920–22. Ref. 1017 AR. A low table with conforming undertier. The tiers are linked by six square columns ringed with ivory. Also made in bur amboina-wood, ash, macassar ebony and oak.

Reuter. Circa 1923. Ref. 1510. AR/1029 NR. Macassar ebony or rosewood. The delicate shagreen-lined top of this table or desk is supported by curious 'double-bell' legs, solid in some versions, veneered in others. The cut-away centre houses a drawer.

Faure. Circa 1925. Ref. 1030 AR/1304 NR. Ruhlmann uses the same 'double-bell' legs for this circular table, this time setting them on a circular base consisting of two discs of Indian rosewood.

Berger. Before 1920. (No reference.) A rustic model; the six small columns supporting the top are attached to a base with four carved feet.

Alimanestiano. Circa 1923. Ref. 1050 NR. A pedestal table which can also be used as a dining table. The solid cylindrical support is flanked by four volutes and has a square entablature.

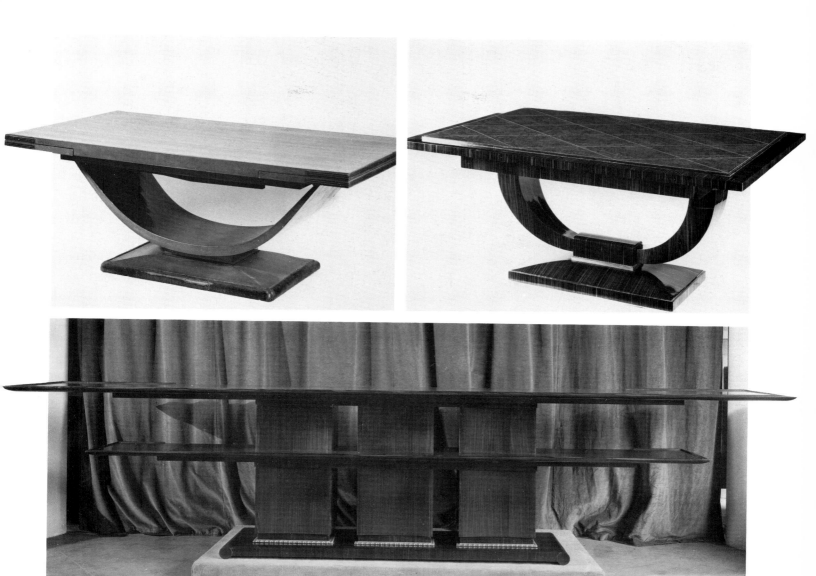

Redhead. 1926. Ref. 1075 AR/1305 NR. Rectangular top with Italianate leaves supported by a cradle standing upon an ogee plinth. Made in satinwood and bur amboina-wood. In some models, the top was lined with shagreen.

Yardley. 1929. Ref. 1403 NR. Made for the English beauty salon. Ruhlmann designed several models of varying lengths, some with two tiers, some with only one. This architectural table has the stream-lined wings of an aircraft.

Vuillerme. 1925–27. Ref 1014 AR/1306 NR. An Italianate table with a top in shagreen or with ivory lattice work. The laterally-placed lyre-base narrows to join the ogee moulded base.

Redhead. Circa 1925. Ref. 1527 AR. This model is similar to a roll-top desk, but has a flatter top. It is cut away at the centre and has two side drawers. The slender legs are inlaid with ivory beading, continuing to the sabots.

Damovale. 1920. Ref. 1529 AR/1602 NR. This lady's desk is almost contemporaneous with the Cabanel model. The sides are slightly rounded to take the curved doors. Top outlined by an ivory dentil. Silk drawer pull. High-placed *fuseau* legs. This model in amaranth or macassar ebony has all the characteristics of Ruhlmann's 'precious' style. Sketches for this piece date back to 1925.

Cabanel. 1919. Ref. 1520 AR/1516 NR. Kidney-shaped desk with two rounded drawers, supported by *fuseau* legs. Filets of ivory divide the veneer (amboina-wood, rosewood, macassar ebony or amaranth) into a diamond pattern. Shagreen medallion in the centre of the top. This model was the prototype for the David-Weill desk.

Vide-poche Fuseaux, c. 1921–22. Ref. 1510 AR. The small sideboard in amaranth, macassar ebony or rosewood with ivory inlays has *fuseau* legs which taper like billiard cues.

Crâne. 1928–29. Ref. 1512 AR/1603 NR. Variation on a roll-top desk, with a narrow waist and no drawers. The trim is in bronze and not ivory.

Salon des Artistes Décorateurs, 1933. Ref. 1600 NR. The last lady's desk, exhibited by Ruhlmann a few months before his death. The frame and legs are in violet-wood, and the morocco-lined body contains a cleverly-contrived set of drawers and pigeonholes. The leaf opens to reveal a writing pad lit by a removable lamp. Presented to the Musée des Arts Décoratifs by Madame Ruhlmann in 1935.

Collectionneur Boudoir. 1925. Ref. 1512 AR/1603 NR. Made in 1922 and first exhibited in 1923, this small desk has a roll top of strips of macassar ebony which, when the lid is closed, look like a section taken through a log. It has the elegance of a Louis XVI desk. Other models in amaranth and American bur walnut. The ivory trim and dentil emphasize the edge of the roll top and the curved line of the legs.

Pilastre/Berger. Circa 1922. Ref. 1039 AR/1514 NR. A flat, architectural desk. The drawers form pilasters and are set back, but broaden to form an ogee moulded base.

Mischer. 1928–29. Ref. 1513 NR. The distinguishing feature of this violet-wood kneehole desk is the shagreen covering with ivory diamonds which extends down over the sides.

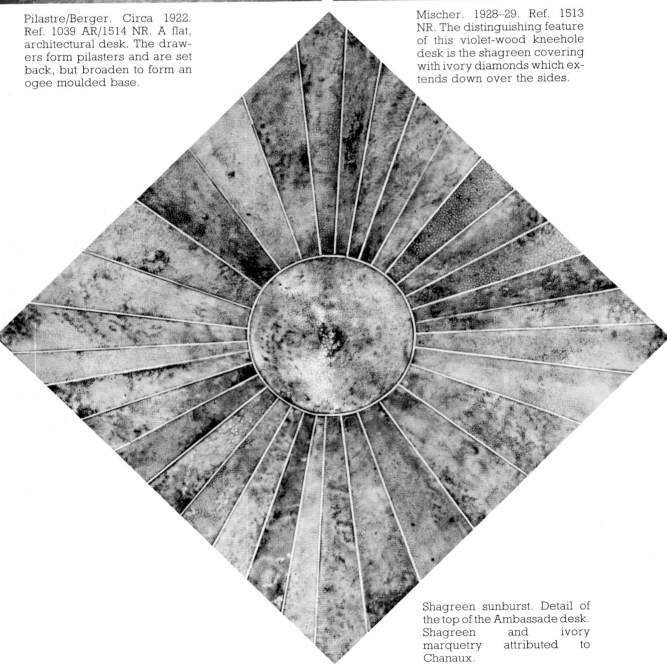

Shagreen sunburst. Detail of the top of the Ambassade desk. Shagreen and ivory marquetry attributed to Chanaux.

Ongule. Circa 1928. Ref. 1545
NR. The name of this rosewood
desk derives from the
(ungulate) shape of the upper
part of the foot.

Dubonnet. A smaller version of
the Ambassade desk (160 ×
85cm as opposed to 175 ×
100cm). American bur walnut,
gilded bronze, top lined in
doeskin.

Collectionneur desk. 1925;
Detail. This is the American
bur walnut version made by
Jules Deroubaix for Monsieur
Schueller in 1929 (470 hours'
work). The upper legs are
fluted, but taper to billiard
cues lower down. Handles and
sabots in ivory. The underside
of the side leaf is cut away to
allow it to slide into the top

Légion d'Honneur. 1930. Ref. 2461 NR. Macassar ebony. Glass doors set in silver-chrome frames. The size of this three-sided display cabinet suggests that it was intended for commercial use.

Bibol Got. Circa 1929. Ref. 2433 NR. Bookcase or display cabinet with three shelves. The supports, in gilded or silvered bronze, are attached to a two-tier flat plinth.

Bibol Stèle. 1933. Ref. 2361 NR. A pair of bookcases in rosewood on plinths designed for the office of André Granet: the last pieces made by Ruhlmann. The only examples are those made for the architect. The silvered bronze reflector masks the source of the indirect lighting.

Van Beuningen. Circa 1930. Ref. 2299 NR. Shown here with a glass door to display collector's pieces, this cabinet has a drawer in the base. It was also made in a version with a solid door decorated with a diamond pattern in ivory. The alabaster plaques are mounted on a bronze listel and conceal strip lights.

Above right: Duval cabinet or *Meuble à chapeau*. 1924. Ref. 1511 AR/2300 NR. An exceptional piece on a macassar ebony base first shown at the 1926 Salon des Artistes Décorateurs in the 'collector's study'. Both doors are veneered with red tortoiseshell with ivory lozenges. The interior, in bur elm, comprises nine identical pigeonholes. Ruhlmann originally designed this piece to store his hats. Twelve copies (an exceptionally large number) were made between 1926 and 1932.

Above and above left: Davène. Circa 1921–29. Ref. 2013 AR/2351 NR. The original model, in either amboina-wood or macassar ebony, had an ivory volute on the recessed pediment and ivory fillets dividing the veneer into squares. A system of wedges allows the height of the shelves to be adjusted, but in theory all the compartments should be of the same size. This piece was made in two sizes: 110 × 158cm and 144 × 180cm.

Standard lamp. Circa 1922. Ref. 3391 NR. The bedside table from the 'Viceroy of India' room transformed into a side table with a lamp concealed in the vase.

Boulard chronometer. Ref. 2024 NR. A unique model commissioned in *c.* 1923.

Haardt easel. 1926. The only distinguishing feature of this display easel is the ogee moulded base.

Travelling mirror. Ref. 3785 NR. Fitted with an inclined support, this macassar ebony mirror is a pocket three-leafed cheval-glass.

Espagnolette. Gilt bronze with a fluted handle. Design by Ruhlmann, made by Fontaine.

Mirror. The mirror has no visible mount and is set in a silver-bronze volute.

Antelope mirror. Circa 1923. A classic model in silver chrome bronze with a slender support that recalls the Antelope wall lamp.

Ref. 3669. Lotus light fitting. Also made with two, three and four fluted branches. Silver bronze. Circa 1925.

Ref. 391. A variation with an alabaster shade.

Ref. 3602. Silver or gilt bronze with opaline glass.

Ref. 3635. *Caillouté* decoration in silver or gilt bronze. Fan-shaped plaque in alabaster.

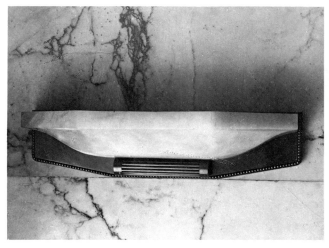

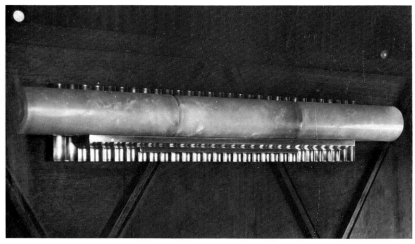

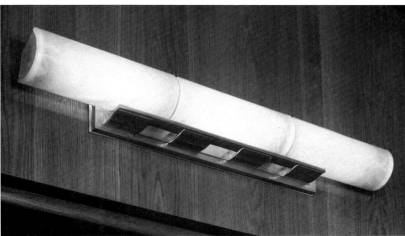

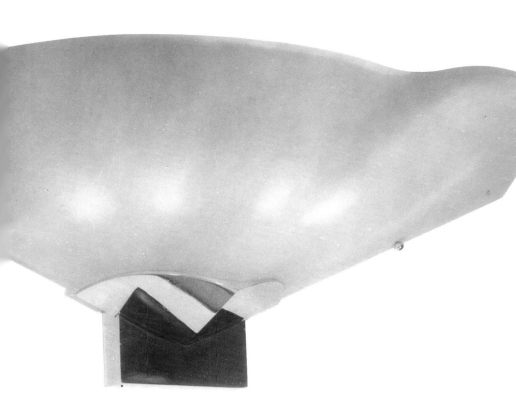

Ref. 3638. Gilt bronze with alabaster edging. This model was used in Ruhlmann's bedroom. Circa 1922.

Ref. 3641. Chrome bronze and alabaster.

Ref. 3691. Three-element alabaster strip light on a fluted silver-bronze wall-mount.

Ref. 3691. Variation with chrome mount.

No reference. Late version of the fan wall lamp.

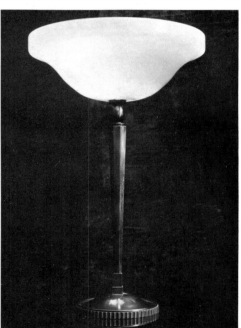

Ref. 3343. Three-branched candelabrum with fluted candle rings. Circa 1922.

Ref. 3316. Table light in silver bronze with alabaster bowl. Before 1930.

Cubical base in solid wood; designed for the Haardt office. 1927.

Ref. 3314. Octagonal base with ribbed stem. Before 1918.

Ref. 3312. One of the earliest models. 1913.

Ref. 3315. Fluted base, with a slender stem supporting an alabaster bowl. Used in Jean Bloch's office in 1926.

Ref. 3377. Large bulbous octagonal base, rising to a fluted ovoid stem. Circa 1920–22.

Ref. 3310A. Spherical vase in craze-finish porcelain by Besnard. 1920 onwards. Used with a different shade on the *Ile de France* (1927).

Ref. 3341. Hexagonal base with pine cone motif. Dish supported by three fluted stems masked by strings of pearls. 1920–22.

Ref. 3304. Ceramic base by Jean Besnard. Prototype for the 'Rendez-vous de pêcheurs de truites'. 1932.

Ref. 298. Gilded bronze with intaglio vermiculated motif. Hemispherical shade in alabaster. 1920 onwards.

Ref. 3634A. A later version without decoration.

No ref. Chromium-plated metal.

No ref. Wall lamp and shade in chromium-plated metal. Office of Monsieur Schueller at L'Oréal.

Ref. 3664. 1913 onwards. Ribbed gilt bronze supporting an alabaster bowl.

Ref. 3664. Wall light with *bouillotte* shade.

Ref. 3633 and 3632. Wall lights for a bathroom: opaline globe and alabaster dish providing indirect lighting.

Ref. 3631. Patinated and gilt bronze with vermiculated pattern.

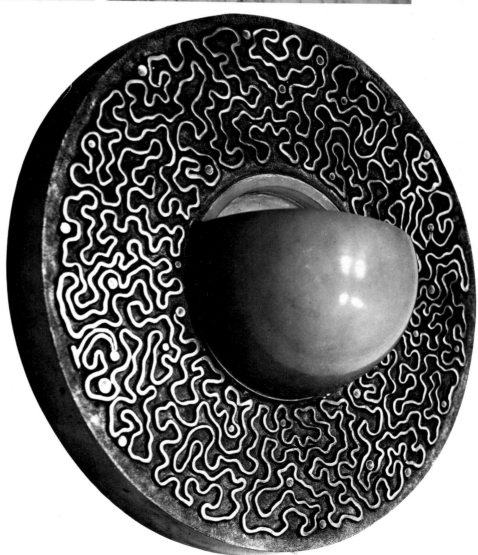

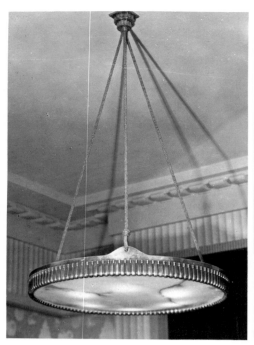

Fluted crown in gilt bronze and alabaster. Circa 1920.

Ref. 3532. Before 1920. The fabric shades around the edge of the dish are somewhat unexpected.

Ref. 3537. Light fitting with two alabaster bowls providing background lighting for a bathroom.

Ref. 4103. Sèvres porcelain and bronze, after a design by Ruhlmann. Made in two sizes. 1926.

Ref. 3540. Chandelier shown at the 1926 Salon des Artistes Décorateurs.

No reference. Chrome and opaline glass.

Ref. 3539. Gilt bronze fittings supported by braids. Alabaster plaques with a number of lighting elements.

Wall light in crystal and gilt bronze from the Hôtel du Collectionneur.

Ref. 3303. Lighting vase from the *Ile de France*.

Stylized geometrical designs in glass developed and executed by Ruhlmann et Laurent. We have already seen that in later years the designer became aware of the architectural and decorative possibilities offered by this material: 'It is translucent and incorruptible. It can be burnished or frosted and can be worked in all sorts of ways. It can be ground or sand-blasted. It can be gilded or silvered, used flat or moulded to any curve.'

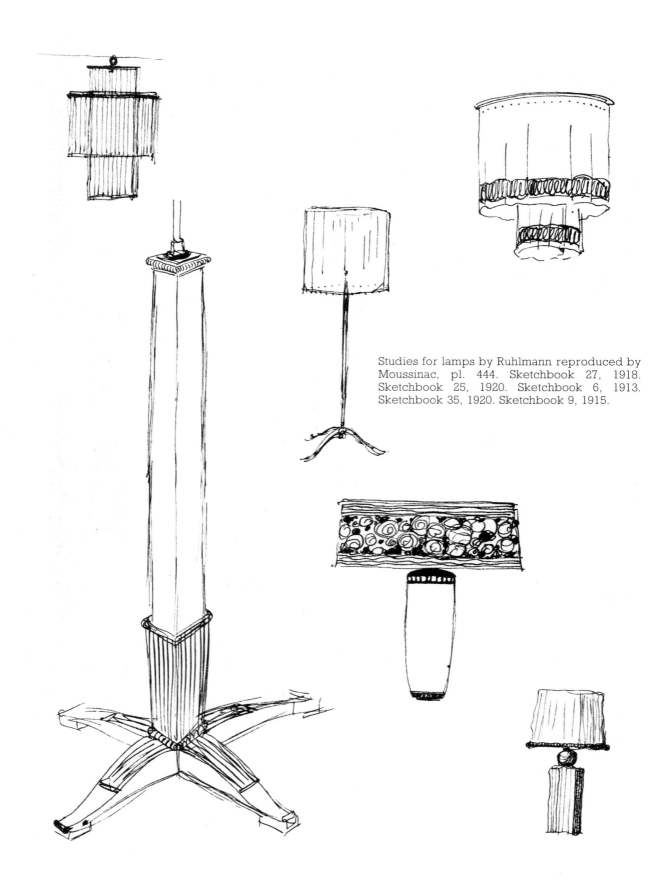

Studies for lamps by Ruhlmann reproduced by
Moussinac, pl. 444. Sketchbook 27, 1918.
Sketchbook 25, 1920. Sketchbook 6, 1913.
Sketchbook 35, 1920. Sketchbook 9, 1915.

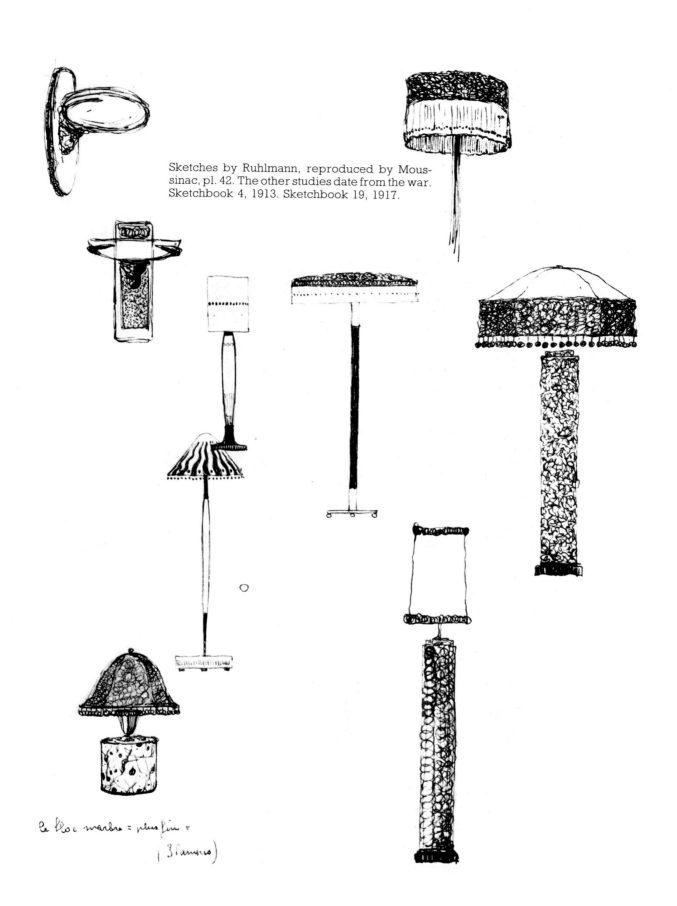

Sketches by Ruhlmann, reproduced by Moussinac, pl. 42. The other studies date from the war. Sketchbook 4, 1913. Sketchbook 19, 1917.

Le bloc marbre = plus fin =
(3 lampes)

Acknowledgments

Our thanks are due to Madame Josette Treffel who kindly made the Ruhlmann archives available, and to Monsieur Jean-Pierre Camard, *expert près la Cour d'Appel*, to Monsieur Pierre Ducharne, Monsieur Henri-Jacques Le Même and Monsieur Jean Rothschild for their valuable help.

Our thanks are also due to all those who talked to us about Jacques-Emile Ruhlmann and helped us to discover his work and life: L'Association pour la commémoration de l'œuvre de Ruhlmann, and in particular Monsieur Paul Beucher, Monsieur Raymond Lautelin, Monsieur Jean-Denis Maclès, Monsieur Maxime Old and Monsieur Noël Porteneuve; Monsieur Pierre Agoune, Madame and Monsieur Bettencourt, Monsieur Mac Le Bot, Monsieur Jean Bounine Cabale, Monsieur André Bronberg, Monsieur Jean-Claude Brugneau, Mr Michael Chow, Monsieur Thierry Couvrat-Devergne, Monsieur Bernard Deloche, Monsieur François Duret-Robert, Monsieur Jean-Jacques Dutko, The Foulke Lewis Gallery, Madame Fraunber, Monsieur Charles Gauthier, Maitre Pierre Hebey, Monsieur Hilten, Monsieur Ithier, Monsieur Alain Jacob, Monsieur Aaron Lederfajn, Monsieur Jacques Lejeune, Monsieur André Leleu, Monsieur Xavier Lenormand, Monsieur Alain Lesieutre, Monsieur Simon Liberman, Monsieur Jean Malgras, Monsieur Félix Marcilhac, Messieurs Marret et Hirt, Monsieur Jacques Mostini, Madame Nathalie Narischkine, Monsieur Marc Pauvarel, Maître Maurice Rheims, Mademoiselle Monique Roland du Noday, Monsieur Gérald Schurr, the Société des Artistes Décorateurs, Société l'Oréal, Madame and Monsieur Valois, Mademoiselle Yvonne Brunhammer, Conservateur at the Musée des Arts Décoratifs, Madame Chantal Bizot, Chargée de Mission at the Musée des Arts Décoratifs, Monsieur Jean Coural, Administrateur Général at the Mobilier National and Madame Anne Lajoie, Conseiller Technique, Madame Penelope Hunter-Stiebel, Metropolitan Museum of New York, Monsieur Jean Adhémar, Conservateur at the Cabinet des Estampes of the Bibliothèque Nationale, and the Société des Amis de la Bibliothèque Forney.

Our grateful thanks are due to the following galleries: Ader-Picard-Tajan, Carayol, Christie's New York (Mr Alastair Duncan and Madame Dominique Stallearts), Deurbergue, Dupuy, Godeau-Audap-Solanet, Langlade, Mathias, Millon, Poulain, Renaud, Le Roux, Sotheby Park Bernet (Madame Sylvie Avizou and Monsieur Philippe Garner).

And to all those who have contributed to the publication of this study.

Photographs: François Boissonnet, Jacques Boulay, Daniel Frasnay, Daniel Mille.

Chronology

1879 Born in Paris on 28 August, son of François Ruhlmann and Valentine Septant.

1900 Meets the well-known architect Pierre Patout while doing his military service. The two later work together and become life-long friends.

1901 Returns to work in his father's business. First furniture designs. Studies landscape painting, a lifelong hobby.

1907 On the death of his father, Ruhlmann takes over the management of Société Ruhlmann. The firm, which specializes in painting, wallpaper and mirrors, is based at 6 rue du Marché Saint-Honoré. Marries Marguerite Seabrook.

1912 Moves to a small building with two entrances: one giving on to rue Maleville, the other on to rue de Lisbonne.

1913 Exhibits furniture, fabrics and lamps at the Salon d'Automne.

1914–18 Declared unfit for military service, Ruhlmann devotes himself to designing furniture.

1919 Founds the firm of Ruhlmann et Laurent.

1920 Becomes *sociétaire* of the Salon d'Automne and a member of the Société des Artistes Décorateurs.

1925 Ruhlmann's highly-acclaimed contribution to the Exposition Internationale des Arts Décoratifs opens up the way for a successful career which will give him an international clientele and bring him major commissions.

1926–27 Ruhlmann is made a Chevalier of the Légion d'Honneur and decorates the debating chamber and ball-room of the Paris Chambre de Commerce.

1927 Decorates the first-class hall (*salon de thé* and games rooms) of the Ile de France.

1929 Furniture designed for the young Maharajah of Indore. Ruhlmann's style begins to move towards a prestigious functionalism.

1932 As a result of the economic crisis, Ruhlmann is obliged to lay off some workers and to cut working hours.

1933 Dies in Paris on 15 November after a sudden illness. Before his death, he orders Ruhlmann et Laurent to be wound up.

Jacques-Emile Ruhlmann at the turn of the century. Charcoal drawing by Degallais, dedicated to 'l'ami Milo', as Ruhlmann was known to close friends.

Signature and authentication

In theory, all Ruhlmann pieces, whether made by outworkers or in his own workshops in the rue d'Ouessant, are stamped with his signature in an inconspicuous place. Chairs made by outside workers are rarely signed, but can be identified from pattern books. The presence of Ruhlmann's stamp is not, however, enough to authenticate a piece. Ruhlmann models made by Porteneuve should bear both their signatures, but some pieces were made 'after Ruhlmann', even during his lifetime. These were made with Ruhlmann's consent by his employees and were for their own use. They are not stamped. After his death, other pieces were made after full-size working drawings. The latter are identifiable only by the fact that they do not conform exactly to the dimensions specified in the pattern books. In his lifetime no outworker would have risked a lawsuit; and Ruhlmann never allowed his cabinet-makers to deviate from his plans by even one centimetre.

Glossary

ajouré term applied to pierced or perforated metalwork

bergère upholstered armchair with rounded back and wide seat

bombé literally, 'blown out'; with a convex swelling

bonheur-du-jour eighteenth-century term for a type of lady's small writing table

bouillotte type of French table lamp

canapé settee or sofa

caillouté pebbled – a type of gilded decoration used in Sèvres porcelain and in marquetry.

causeuse type of small *canapé* or large chair for two people

chaise-*gondole* type of armchair with a deep rounded back

chiffonier piece of furniture for the storage of stuffs and small pieces of clothing; usually a small, low chest of drawers

ébénisterie cabinet-making. The *ébéniste* specialized in veneered furniture, as distinct from the *menuisier* (or joiner) who specialized in carved pieces in plain woods

entre-deux to be placed between two windows

espagnolette the hinged fastening used on double French doors and windows

fuseau, fuseau à facettes type of furniture leg designed by Ruhlmann – see p. 50

guéridon candlestand or small table suitable for holding a candelabrum

lampas figured textile, similar to damask in appearance but heavier

listel small border or fillet

méridienne type of *canapé* with one end higher than the other

réchampi ornamentation picked out in gold or in a colour different from the ground

sabot metal shoe enclosing the bottom of the leg of a piece of furniture

stèle upright slab

tapis covering on a desk or table top

vasque large shallow basin

vide-poche small bedroom table with a deeply rimmed top, designed to hold the contents of a man's pockets when he undresses

Bibliography

'L'Avenir du luxe', *Heim*, September 1932.

'Ruhlmann ébéniste et décorateur des Années 20', *Connaissance des arts*, February 1960.

' Ruhlmanisme', *Art Présent*, 1947.

'Le Théâtre de la Michodière', *Le Théâtre et Comoedia illustré*, January 1926.

Badovici, *Harmonies. Intérieurs de Ruhlmann*, A. Morancé Editeur, Paris, 1924.

De Beauplan, 'Une Réalisation nouvelle de décoration théâtrale, *Christine*', *L'Illustration*, December 1932.

D'Alnois, 'La rétrospective Ruhlmann au Pavillon de Marsan', *Plaisir de France*, July 1935.

Besnard, 'Quelques nouveaux meubles de Ruhlmann', *Art et décoration*, March 1924.

Deshairs, *L'Hôtel du Collectionneur*, Albert Véry Editeur, Paris, 1926.

'Une Etape vers le meuble métallique', *Art et décoration*, March 1924.

Dayot, 'J.E. Ruhlmann', *L'Art et les artistes*, January 1935.

Fréchet, 'Ruhlmann', *Mobilier et décoration d'intérieur*, February–March 1924.

Forthuny, 'Réponse de Ruhlmann à l'enquête sur la venue des Allemands à l'Exposition des Arts Décoratifs', *L'Amour de l'art*, 1922, pp. 61–62.

Goissaud, 'L'Hôtel du Collectionneur', *La Construction moderne*, January 1926.

Hunter-Stiebel, 'Art Déco and the Metropolitan Museum of Modern Art', *The Connoisseur*, April 1972.

Janneau, 'D'André-Charles Boulle à Ruhlmann', *Revue de l'Art*, December 1934.

Lahalle, 'L'Oeuvre de Ruhlmann et le Paquebot Ile de France', *Mobilier et décoration d'intérieur*, 1927, pp. 147–153.

Laran, 'Notre enquête sur le mobilier moderne, J.E. Ruhlmann', *Art et décoration*, January 1920.

Le Fèvre, 'A l'Exposition des Arts Décoratifs', *L'Art vivant*, July 1925.

Moussinac, *Harmonies: Intérieurs de Ruhlmann*, A. Morancé Editeur, Paris, 1924.

Roger-Marx, 'La Rétrospective Ruhlmann', *L'Europe nouvelle*, November 1934.

De Rudder, 'Ruhlmann, le sage des Anneés Folles', *L'Estampille*, January 1970.

Varagnac, 'Une Evolution nouvelle du mobilier', *L'Amour de l'art*, 1920.

Vaillat, 'L'Art décoratif et l'esthétique d'un grand paquebot', *L'Illustration*, 18 June 1927.

Varenne, 'Une Ensemble de Ruhlmann à la Chambre de Commerce de Paris', *Art et décoration*, 1928, p. 9.

Zahar, 'Oeuvres dernières de Ruhlmann', *Art et décoration*, January 1934.

Exhibition catalogues

Exposition Internationale des Arts Décoratifs et Industriels Modernes, Paris, 1925.
Le Décor et la vie de 1900 à 1925, Pavillon de Marsan, Paris, 1937.
Les Années 25, Musée des Arts Décoratifs, Paris, 1966.
The World of Art Déco, Minneapolis Institute of Art, 1971.
1925. Exposition du Cinquantenaire. Sous la direction d'Yvonne Brunhammer, Presses de la Connaissance, Paris, 1976.
1930. Quand le meuble devient sculpture, Louvre des Antiquaires, Paris, 1981.
Rétrospective Ruhlmann, Pavillon de Marsan, 1934.
Ruhlmann Centenary Exhibition, The Foulke Lewis Collection, London, 1979.

Aesthetics and Furniture: books and articles

Collective, *Le Meuble. La Tradition française*, Editions du Chêne, Paris, 1941.
Baudrillard, *Le Système des objets*, Collection Médiation, Paris, 1972.
Deloche, *L'Art du meuble. Introduction à l'esthétique des arts mineurs*, L'Hermès, Lyon, 1980.
Janneau, *Le Mobilier français*, P.U.F., Paris, 1941.
L'Ebénisterie, Editions Fréal, Paris, 1974.
Kheim, *Le Beau meuble de France*, Nilsson, Paris, c.1926, Tome 8.
Sedeyn, *Le Mobilier. L'Art français depuis vingt ans*, Paris, Editions Rieder, 1921.
Varenne, 'La Technique moderne de l'ébénisterie', *Art et décoration*, 1927.
Viaux, *Le Meuble en France*, P.U.F., Paris, 1962.
Viaux, *Bibliographie du meuble*, Société des Amis de la Bibliothèque Forney, 1966.

Modern Decorative Arts and Furniture

Encyclopédie visuelle des arts 1890–1940. Collectif sous la direction de Maître M. Rheims, Elsevier, Bordas Editeur, Paris, 1981.
Arwas, *Art Déco*, Academy Editions, London, 1980.
Badovici, *Intérieurs de Sue et Mare*, A. Morancé Editeur, Paris, 1924.
Battersby, *The Decorative Twenties*, Studio Vista, London, 1969.
Battersby, *The Decorative Thirties*, Studio Vista, London, 1971.
Brunhammer, *Le Style 1925*, Baschet Editeur, Paris, 1975.
Bizot and Mannoni, *Mobilier 1900–1925*, Massin Editeur, Paris.
Dufrêne, *Les Arts décoratifs modernes*.
Hillier, *Art Déco of the Twenties and Thirties*, London, 1968.
Janneau, *Technique du décor intérieur moderne*, A. Morancé Editeur, Paris.
Formes Nouvelles, programme nouveau, Paris, 1926.
Meubles et Décors – Retour aux traditions 1910–1925, Paris, 1966.
Kjellberg, *Art Déco. Les Maîtres du mobilier*, Editions de l'amateur, 1981.
Le Corbusier, *L'Art décoratif d'aujourd'hui*, Collection 'Esprit Nouveau', Crès, Paris, 1925.
Leleu, 'Où en est l'art décoratif moderne?', special issue of *Art et décoration*, March 1948.
Lesieutre, *The Spirit and Splendour of Art Déco*, Paddington Press, 1975.
Mourey, *L'Art décoratif en France de la Révolution à nos jours*, Paris, 1925, Tome 4.
Essai sur l'art décoratif français moderne, Ollendorf, Paris, 1921.
Morrison McClinton, *Art Déco, A Guide for Collectors*, Clarkson Potter, New York, 1973.
Olmer, *Le mobilier français d'aujourd'hui, 1910–1925*, Van Oest, Paris, 1926.
Quenioux, *Les Arts décoratifs modernes*, Larousse, Paris, 1925.
Tixier, *Les Arts décoratifs 1920–1930*, Société des amis de la bibliothèque Forney.
Verlet, *Styles, meubles, décors de Louis XVI à nos jours*, Larousse, Paris, 1972, Tome 2.
Verne and Chavance, *Pour comprendre l'art décoratif moderne en France*, Hachette, Paris, 1925.
Veronesi, *Into the Twenties*, Thames and Hudson, London, 1968.

Index

Acknowledgments to private collections

page
34 Cheval glass: formerly Deroubaix
35 Rodier bar: Hervé Poulain Triplan secretaire: Galerie Valois, formerly Clarisse Neimann
38 Make-up cabinet: Felix Marcilhac
57 Nicolle drinks cabinet: Felix Marcilhac
181 Soleil bed: Hervé Aaron, New York
249 Sanders bed: Felix Marcilhac
266 Crédit Foncier chair: Felix Marcilhac
273 Dunand/Collectionneur sideboard: formerly Felix Marcilhac
277 Colette and Grande cannelée . . . commodes: Felix Marcilhac
283 Araignée and Colonnettes tables: Felix Marcilhac
291 Davene bookcase: Felix Marcilhac